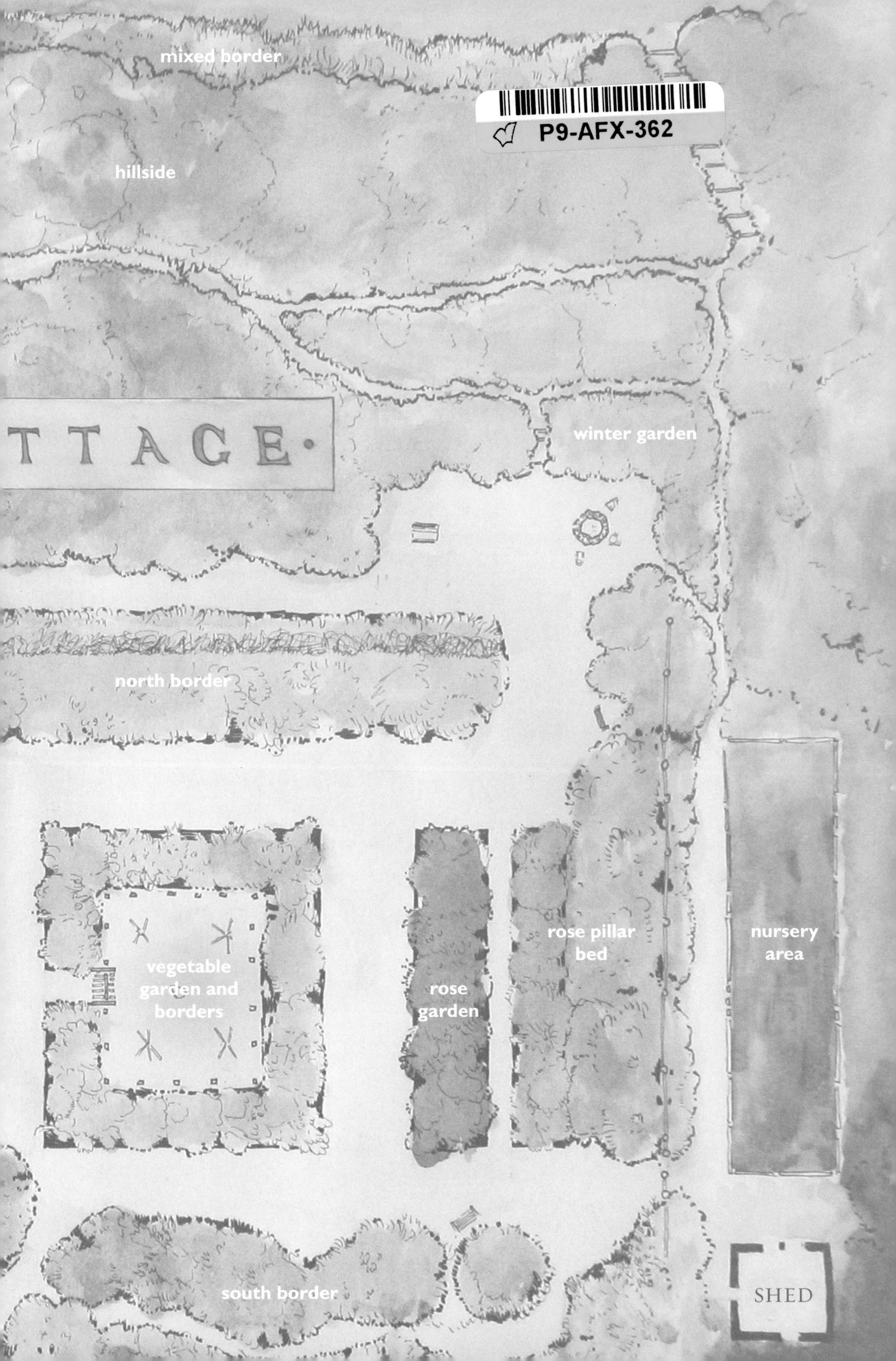

mixed border

hillside

TTAGE·

winter garden

north border

rose pillar
bed

nursery
area

vegetable
garden and
borders

rose
garden

south border

SHED

The LAYERED GARDEN

DAVID L. CULP

with Adam Levine

PHOTOGRAPHS BY ROB CARDILLO

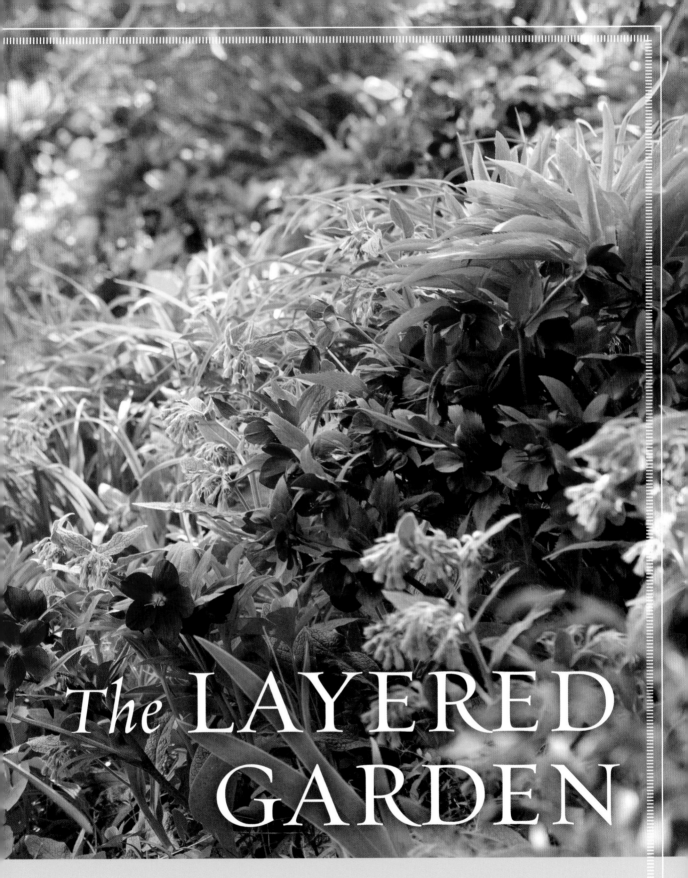

The LAYERED GARDEN

DESIGN LESSONS FOR YEAR-ROUND
BEAUTY FROM BRANDYWINE COTTAGE

TIMBER PRESS
Portland, Oregon

To Michael Scott Alderfer,
Joanna Reed, *and* Dennis West

and to my mother and father

Frontispiece: A spring view of the hillside mixed border.

Opposite: A selection of blossoms of my 'Brandywine Hybrid' hellebores reveals the stunning allure and spectacular colors of these distinctive winter-blooming plants.

Next page: *Wisteria frutescens* is not invasive like the Asian forms of the genus, and in some years it will rebloom.

Endpaper illustration by Adrian Martinez
Book design by Laura Shaw Design

Published in 2012 by Timber Press, Inc.

The Haseltine Building
133 S.W. Second Avenue, Suite 450
Portland, Oregon 97204-3527
timberpress.com

Printed in China
Fourth printing 2015

Library of Congress Cataloging-in-Publication Data

Culp, David L.
   The layered garden: design lessons for year-round beauty from Brandywine Cottage/David L. Culp; with Adam Levine; photographs by Rob Cardillo.—1st ed.
       p. cm.
   Includes bibliographical references and index.
   ISBN 978-1-60469-236-5
   1. Gardens—Pennsylvania—Design. 2. Gardening—Pennsylvania—Anecdotes. I. Levine, Adam. II. Cardillo, Rob. III. Title.
   SB473.C84 2012
   635.09748—dc23   2012007640

A catalog record for this book is also available from the British Library.

"I do hold it in the royal ordering of gardens, there ought to be gardens for all months in the year, in which, severally, things of beauty may be then in season."

—FRANCIS BACON,
"Of Gardens," 1625

CONTENTS

IF YOU ARE READING THIS, YOU HAVE PROBABLY already been intrigued and seduced by the beauty glimpsed while looking through this book. Maybe you studied the table of contents, and noticed that the book is chock full of practical information to complement its visual enticement. Or perhaps you are lucky enough to know David Culp and his garden, or someone who does told you to get this book.

All good reasons, and there are more. Books by great gardenmakers that combine design inspiration, plantsmanship, and practical information are few and far between. And those that do it in a welcoming manner straight from experience and from the heart, even fewer yet. For readers seeking advice on garden design, be they setting out on making their first garden or wondering how to transform an existing one into something as complex, beautiful, and ever-changing year-round as David's garden at Brandywine Cottage, depicted so richly in the photographs, this book will inspire and teach. And for the many seasoned gardeners who find it increasingly difficult to manage our plant obsessions and collector's impulses with aesthetic goals for our gardens, this is the book to read.

As an apostle to abundance and diversity yet also to overall beauty, David explores and explains his layering technique and how it allows him to keep experimenting with "how much beauty and pleasure I can wring out of a space." By taking the reader on a journey of how he created and continues to change and tend his immensely plant-rich garden, we see the ways he and we can orchestrate seasonal moments and color progressions, vivify and showcase our favorite plants, deal with their inevitable lapses, and find gracious ways to integrate yet more of the plants that have been winners and new plants that we desire. Specific plants and practical advice are threaded throughout. For me, a reluctant reader who would much rather learn by doing, this book is a revelation in how to cover an immense amount of minute details as well as general overarching ideas without making readers feel like they are being taught. It is like a more organized and comprehensive version of spending one day a month for an entire year at David's side, helping while he goes about gardening, with him talking to you the entire time.

As his many fans and friends know, David Culp is an American treasure. It is difficult to wrest this man away from his passions—plants, gardening, and sharing with people. This is a man of intuition, warmth, optimism, generosity, and incredible energy and work ethic. He is a gardener and designer who learns by doing and by connecting with others as much as or more than by studying and drafting. Readers are fortunate he has finally found time to write this book. What also sets this book apart are the at-times humorous and often moving glimpses into David's gentle, thoughtful, and humble philosophies on gardening and on life. I'm certain that the only reason he has created this superb tome, aside from exhortations from friends and colleagues, is that his life is one of doing and sharing, and the act of writing a book—no matter how daunting and tedious—fits that description as well as do all the other things David takes on.

For these reasons, this book is destined to be a classic. But it is also uniquely modern. David is a man who has preceded current trends in sustainability by, as he puts it, "living and working within our means and leaving a light footprint on the land." He has wanted to nourish the web of life since a child, and his wildlife-friendly, site-adapted practices ring

Previous: A bright May morning lights up the borders around the picket-fenced vegetable garden.

10   FOREWORD

all the more true in this day and age of heightened awareness of the need to use and steward thoughtfully. And, on a lighter note, he has raised vegetables and chickens and made a roof garden long before they returned to the public consciousness and became popular obsessions.

David understands and eloquently describes making the connection of a garden to its site, house, and to the natural and cultural aspects of its region—creating a sense of place. He also deeply feels the importance of the connection of a garden to its maker's past, family and friends, forebears, and to the gardenmaker himself or herself. He is a man who is joined to the past with respect and gratitude, who lives with passion and pleasure in the present, and who looks forward with curiosity and hope to the future. His garden and his words reflect this, making this book also a book on how to live life, with a garden or without. Even a nongardener will come away inspired by this man's kind and generous view of the world (and probably also inspired to start a first garden).

Gardenmaking, in its finest form, is a celebration of life and of love. David and this book epitomize this. Reading his words and seeing images of his garden, you will learn, be inspired, and enjoy.

LAUREN SPRINGER OGDEN
December 2011

ONE FALL WHEN I WAS ABOUT NINE, MY
Grandmother Thorpe gave me a bag of bulbs and
said, "You go out and plant them." I felt more than a little
trepidation—I had never planted anything without her
supervision—but she reassured me, "You can do it. You won't
go wrong!" Her generosity could have been ruinous to her
flower border, but I got the bulbs planted with no mishaps.
The next spring, when they bloomed, I almost burst with
pride when she told all her friends, "David did that!" From
that moment I knew I was a gardener, and after all these
years it remains the core of how I define myself.

More than anything else in my career, I want to do what my grandmother did for me: empower people to garden. This is a large part of why I lecture around the country, why I have taught at Longwood Gardens for many years, why we open our garden to the public for tours, why I have become an active member in numerous plant societies—and why I wanted to write this book. People say I am a good horticulturist, but I also feel I am a good horticultural cheerleader, since I always try to emphasize the cheer. The path to horticultural enlightenment may be littered with countless missteps, mistakes, and (may I be honest?) dead plants. But the wonder of gardening is that it always keeps us looking forward, since there is always the next flower to bloom, the next season, next year.

When my Grandmother Culp moved from near Pittsburgh to St. Petersburg, Florida, her roses went with her. Even though the plants struggled in that too-warm climate, she told me that she loved roses too much to ever do without them. Her passion for plants has become my passion. Perhaps it is also because of her that I am an undaunted gardener. Telling me I cannot grow a particular plant is a sure way to get me to try it.

Rather than focusing on limitations, I prefer to dwell in the much more pleasant realm of possibilities. When I look at a particular genus, I see all the possibilities embraced within it: the range of colors, sizes, forms, and seasons of bloom. When I see a particular piece of ground, I am always asking how many plants I can fit there, how much beauty and pleasure I can wring out of that space. I have learned over time that *no* is rarely the right answer; with energy and ingenuity, almost any question can be answered with *yes*.

Yet I need to add that patience is truly a virtue, because time is one of a gardener's greatest allies. With the passage of time, plants grow and our instincts and abilities as gardeners mature and improve. Nothing happens in an instant in the garden; beautiful moments always unfold on their own schedule, in their own sweet time. We may savor that sweetness, and remember it for the rest of our lives. But for anyone who loves gardens, it also helps to love being a gardener, since it is only the continuum of day-to-day work that makes those moments possible.

Previous: An April view of the hillside mixed border.

Opposite: We grow many tender plants in containers. In this example, *Eucomis comosa* 'Sparkling Burgundy', with its striking purple stem, is grown beside *Euphorbia* ×*martinii* 'Ascot Rainbow', a plant whose color is very useful in combinations.

The PATH to BRANDYWINE COTTAGE

GARDENING OFTEN BRINGS ME TO MY KNEES. By this I mean more than the planting, weeding, and fussing, the bended-knee, manicure-destroying grunt work that all of us do. The beauty and diversity of plants often stop me in my tracks, and I am never satisfied to simply gaze at these wonders from above. I get down on my knees to get a closer look, touching the plants and the soil they grow in, a communion that connects me to the earth and to life on Earth in an immediate, almost electric way. Many of my favorite flowers are tiny, their differences minute and

seemingly inconsequential to the average observer, but I love examining all the facets of their intricate beauty. I especially love when someone kneels beside me, so I can share my fascination with a kindred spirit. Over a lifetime of varied horticultural pursuits, I have learned that the closer I look, the more astounded I become, and the more in love I fall with plants and the gardens in which they reside.

I have been a passionate plantsman and collector since I was a child, and Brandywine Cottage, the 2-acre garden I tend with Michael Alderfer in southeastern Pennsylvania, is home to unusual plants from all over the world. The collector in me thinks each individual specimen is beautiful, of course; otherwise I would not bother growing them. But the designer in me wants more than a botanical garden with each genus grown in its separate bed. Plants are the basis of my garden artistry, serving as pieces in a design puzzle, as colors in a palette, as elements of a sculpture. As with artists in any medium, the more we learn about these vehicles for our expression and the more passionate we are about them, the more ways we will find to use them and the more beautiful our gardens will become.

Combining plants in a multitude of ways, based on their habits and moods, how they live and even how they die, gives my garden successive layers of interest that extend into every month of the year. I use the term "layers" as shorthand for a design process by which I try to maximize the beauty and interest from each planted space, by combining complementary plants that either grow and bloom together or follow each other in succession. While succession planting is part of this design approach, my idea of layering goes beyond just the plants to encompass the development of each bed and how the beds relate to each other and the garden as a whole. More than just making sure one blooming plant follows another, layering is the art of creating a series of peak garden moments, the anticipation of which gets me out of bed in the morning.

Trying to describe something visual in words is like trying to write about the taste of a complex food. How would you describe the taste of a curry? I could list all the spices that go into it, come up with a few adjectives like hot and spicy, but none of this would tell you exactly how it makes you feel when you first taste it. A layered garden like mine is complex, like a curry, with depths that are not all apparent at first glance and which can be savored in many ways, at many levels. My hellebores can be seen as simply beautiful; but my hellebore breeding can be an exercise in mathematical probability that I will explain to anyone who wants to listen. And in my layered garden, my hellebore bed is more than just hellebores: otherwise why would I want to look at it once these flowers were done blooming? Layering allows me to use all the many plants I collect in exciting ways that highlight the individuals while melding the collections into a coherent and cohesive whole.

Countless people have provided me with the ideas that, sifted and composted in my mind, ended up in the ground at the Brandywine Cottage garden. Not all gardens are designed in layers, but layering is a feature of many of the gardens I love and is practiced by many of the gardeners I admire. I certainly make no claim that the "layered garden" (or anything else in this book) is my own invention. What I hope to offer, in the text and especially in the photographs and captions, is an intimate look at how one such garden has been conceived and constructed. Just as we can learn much by the peering into individual flowers, the close examination of any good garden, along with insights into the minds and the methods of its gardeners, can teach many lessons.

Before getting into the specifics of creating a layered garden, I want to relate how I became a gardener, and how the garden at Brandywine Cottage came to be. I cannot remember a time in my life when I did not have plants of my own. I was no more than five years old when I first heard the "Jack and the Beanstalk" story, which inspired me to plant bean seeds in paper cups so that, like Jack, I could climb my vine into the sky. I planted pumpkin seeds in a Dutch Masters cigar box one year, doing this after Halloween, and it mattered little to me that my timing was off. I simply enjoyed watching things grow. To this day, the magic of planting a seed and seeing it emerge from the soil never fails to amaze me.

My parents and grandparents all had gardens—vegetable beds as well as flower borders—and even as a little kid, everything outdoors fell into my realm. Everyone around the neighborhood knew that "David has a knack for growing things." People would call to ask if I could plant such

and such for them, insisting that my green thumb would get their plants off to a better start, and I fell for this flattery every time. Only later did I wonder if these folks might have also been using me as an unwitting source of free labor. In any case, I loved plants then as much as I do now, so these chores were always fun. By third or fourth grade I was wandering into neighbors' gardens, wide-eyed, asking questions about their plants and how they grew them. I have done this ever since; the only difference is that now I carry a notebook.

During summer vacations when I was a little boy, my mother and I would take the train from our home in Reading, Pennsylvania, to her parents' farm in the Great Smoky Mountains of Tennessee. I delighted in these visits, begging to stay as long as possible, and the happiest times were when I spent all summer there. My family moved to Tennessee when I was ten, and the farm and mountains became more easily accessible. At my grandparents' place I had my own pony and calf and chickens, and my own garden beds. The surrounding woods and fields and streams were my extended playground, where I learned to identify ferns and wildflowers, edible greens and berries, and fell in love with the natural world. I never wanted those summers to end and, in some ways, they have not.

When in high school, I made pocket money working in a neighbor's garden, finally getting paid for the work that I once gladly did for free. After graduating from college with a degree in psychology, I moved to Atlanta. I pursued a career in retail while helping restore an old house there, but developing the gardens around that house became my focus.

Friends and neighbors soon asked me to do garden designs for them; some even suggested I change careers. Nursery catalogs and garden books became my favorite reading material, and I continued my lifelong habit of visiting gardens and asking questions. I moved to another old house in Matthews, North Carolina, about twelve miles outside Charlotte, where I grew camellias, hellebores, German iris, old roses, and learned from wonderful gardener-neighbors while working for a wholesale florist. I moved back to Pennsylvania in 1988 and got a job at Waterloo Gardens, a retail nursery in the Philadelphia suburbs, where I became their perennial buyer and continued my on-the-job education while also taking horticulture courses at Temple University. A few years later I took a job in sales and plant research and development for Sunny Border Nurseries in Kensington, Connecticut, where I now serve as vice president.

Having grown up in Pennsylvania, I loved the pastoral feel of the land, the gentle rolling hills, the simple domestic architecture. The region has a history of horticulture that goes back hundreds of years, and it is home to more public gardens than almost anyplace in the country. This was a fertile place for a soul like me to be.

While looking for just the right house, I shared an apartment with a "hope chest" of plants I had brought from my North Carolina garden. This collection filled the apartment balcony, the entire spare bedroom, and a clearing in the woods nearby. These plants needed somewhere to put down roots, and so did I. It took two years of searching, but when I finally found the house I now call Brandywine Cottage in 1990, I knew it was the place. Even before I owned the property, I dreamed about the garden I might make on that land.

Like so many people in the first throes of love, I had failed to take into account the faults of my beloved—the poison ivy, multiflora rose, and Japanese honeysuckle that infested the hillside, the peeling paint and other problems with the old house itself, and the residential development that quickly sprang up on the subdivided remnants of the farm that my property had been part of. Each of these challenges was dealt with in time. But in the beginning, none of this mattered, because really, it was more than just love at first sight. This simple farmhouse, built in the 1790s, struck a chord that reached back to my ancestors. The solidness of the stucco-on-stone structure and its simplicity of line felt right for a Pennsylvania native returning to his home soil after more than twenty years in the South. I loved how the white house sat nestled on the land, sheltered on the lee side of a hill—just like the white house on my grandparent's farm.

In creating our gardens, I think we often look back, sometimes unconsciously, to our early sense of what is beautiful. My ideal, a bucolic combination of the pastoral and the wild, was formed during my childhood summer vacations. Over the past twenty years, Michael and I have managed to imbue the wooded hillside acre of the property with some of the wildness that I loved to romp in as a boy, while the flat open acre on which the house sits has the pastoral feel of a miniature farm. The Culp family came here as farmers more than 300 years ago, the Alderfers almost as long ago, and we continue that heritage today, living in an old farmhouse, keeping a garden, both of us making a living by working with plants.

Unlike some gardening partners, Michael and I garden together. From the beginning, we thought it best not to have separate areas of the garden, so visitors to Brandywine Cottage find no dividing lines demarcating particular spaces. He moved in three years after I bought the house, and his love of plants, his hard work, and our individual and shared visions for the garden have made it what it is.

Like me, Michael was a child gardener, helping with the planting and maintenance of his parents' property. We both come from Pennsylvania Dutch (more properly called German Anabaptist) backgrounds and share similar values, including a respect for the land. He loves planting things, which is fortunate considering the number of plants that follow me home. For the past twenty years, he has tended interior plantscapes for museums, public buildings, private homes, and other clients, and those skills carry over to home, where he tends our houseplants, and creates colorful seasonal outdoor containers and indoor flower arrangements year-round.

Our lack of dividing lines helps give the garden a unity of design, but of course this also leads to occasional disagreements on how things should be done. These disagreements, in turn, lead to interesting "discussions," but the common ground we eventually reach is well worth it. Since the garden we have created together is far too large for one person to care for by himself, we try to be grateful for any job that gets done, even if one of us may have approached it a different way. And at the end of the day, I feel happier and more secure knowing that my passion for this place is not just my own—that there is another living being who cares as deeply about Brandywine Cottage as I do.

CHAPTER ONE

The LAYERED GARDEN

THE GARDEN AT BRANDYWINE COTTAGE WAS NOT created in a month or even in the first year or two. While I knew I could make a wonderful garden on that appealing piece of land, it did not come to me all at once. I had created several other gardens in my adult life, and I knew it would take years to make the garden of my dreams a reality. I also knew it would end up being different from the dreams, because reality is less forgiving and dreams change over time. Even if I had been able to conjure up a complete picture immediately, I still would have wanted to take the time to let it unfold, and to do the work myself.

A garden like ours, in which there are layers of interest in every month of the year—even flowers to cut for indoor arrangements—is not a common achievement in the temperate climate (USDA zone 6) of my region, where freezing temperatures keep most gardeners indoors from November through March. More common in that area are what I call "big bang" gardens, which feature extravagant floral displays that begin in the spring and wane in midsummer. By then gardeners often feel as burned out as their plants, and might even be praying for an early frost so they can be done with it until the next spring.

For Michael and me, frost simply means the start of another gardening season. It is a slower season, for sure, a time for a final cleanup of the borders, dealing with hardscape problems, doing necessary pruning and other chores that we failed to get to during the garden's peak seasons. Even with snow on the ground, we can be cleaning and sharpening tools and getting the shed organized, which is more than just busywork. Working during the usual gardener's downtime makes everything go more smoothly when the rush of outdoor chores arrives—a rush that begins for us when the winter layer of the garden begins to pop in February, months earlier than the usual April start time for most of our gardening neighbors.

Since we never really stop working, sometimes I am not even sure which garden season I am tending. Take my crocuses and snowdrops, for instance: in March, *Crocus tommasinianus* might be blooming with *Galanthus elwesii*; in fall the combination might be *Crocus pulchellus* and *Galanthus* 'Potter's Prelude'. So the question is, are those spring crocuses and snowdrops the first of the year to bloom in my garden, or the last? I do not have an answer to that chicken-egg question, but since our gardening year never ends, it really does not matter. Our garden is a living-growing-dying art form, always unfolding, always changing—an unfinished rhapsody that we continue to edit and refine as the seasons come and go, as plants grow and die, and as new ideas and obsessions are added to the mix.

GETTING TO KNOW THE
LAYERED GARDEN CONCEPT

The key to creating a many-layered garden is understanding and taking advantage of the ways plants grow and change through the seasons and over the years, providing different textures, colors, and effects and evoking a variety of feelings. Garden layers are made up of a variety of plants, some with complementary or contrasting colors, others with interesting shapes or textures. Layers are more than just perennials, or annuals, or bulbs, or groundcovers—they are more than just the ground layer of plants that is the sole focus of many gardeners. Beautiful combinations are certainly possible, even on the tiniest scale: dwarf Solomon's seal

Previous: Staddle stones like this one were once used as supports to raise granaries off the ground to protect them from rats and other pests. Such an ornament fits my criterion of garden art being largely utilitarian.

Opposite, top and bottom: We see this view of the hillside every day when we go in and out of the house, so the combinations need to be both pleasing and change with the seasons. The two photographs were taken in early spring about three weeks apart.

underplanted with moss certainly makes a precious 6-inch-high picture. But to get the most interest from any garden, all the layers need to be considered, from the ground level to the middle level of shrubs, and small trees up to the canopy trees. Growing plants on vertical surfaces—walls, fences, trellises, arbors, and other supports, even climbing up trees when we can be sure they will do no harm—adds to the picture by bringing flowers and foliage to eye level and above.

I also consider entire beds, or even entire garden sections, as layers unto themselves. My hillside, which looks like a tilted canvas when viewed from below, could be considered a layer, while the flat area around the house is another layer. These areas in turn are divided into smaller and smaller spaces, right down to the level of three-plant combinations—as when I underplant witch hazel (*Hamamelis ×intermedia* 'Pallida') with a yellow *Galanthus* cultivar and winter aconite (*Eranthis hyemalis*), with the yellow of the witch hazel flowers reflected in the plants on the ground.

Our garden at Brandywine Cottage has been designed so that different areas peak at different times: For example, when the hillside is at its height of bloom in early spring, the borders below are barely breaking dormancy, and when the borders peak later in spring, the hillside has entered a quieter phase. Most areas have more than one peak. The hillside puts on a second show when hydrangeas bloom, and a third show with colorful fall foliage; the ruin wall goes through several waves of bloom; and the borders offer a series of waves that carry on until frost.

Opposite: This June view, looking into the ruin garden from the deck above, shows how every layer is used, from the ground-hugging plants to the taller plants to those growing in the wall, on to the trees and shrubs behind the wall. The ruin garden was created in the ruins of the barn's stable on the property.

This page: One way I try to make the seasons last longer is by extending the bloom time of favorite plants. I have expanded my collection of narcissus to include both early and late blooming varieties, such as **(left)** *Narcissus cyclamineus*, shown in late March, and **(right)** *N.* 'Pipit' in late April.

I would not be happy with a garden in which everything bloomed at once. From a gardener's point of view, I would have little motivation to do any work once that peak had passed. And from a design point of view, it would be like listening to a cacophony rather than a symphony—which, like my garden, has its crescendos, its quiet spaces, and its movements, all carefully composed. Each section has multiple layers of interest, sometimes working in concert and at other times playing off each other. It is the gradual, suspenseful revelation of the composition—the hallmark of any good piece of art—that I find most exciting. The only difference is that the occasional mournful adagios in a garden are never planned, only dealt with in the aftermath, and often sadder than any music can be.

If my garden is a symphony, I hope I have made it a romantic one. I want my garden to seduce me, to draw me in, to make me forget about the rest of the world as long as it holds me under its spell. Even though I have no children, I understand why my grandmother expressed such

pleasure whenever she had all the family around. I like to have all my plants around, to be surrounded and embraced by those I love.

One other garden layer—or maybe garden player is a better term—is the passage of time. After twenty years spent gardening the same space, it seems that times does go by faster now, maybe because I am always pushing the seasons, always looking ahead to the next thing. When I started the garden, I was so anxious to see things come into bloom that I always picked the earliest blooming cultivars. Now, as I am growing older along with the garden, I have learned the rewards of stretching out each season as far as I can, by adding the late bloomers of a genus to the mix. I started with an early rhododendron, *Rhododendron mucronulatum*, and now I plant late-blooming native azaleas. To my plantings of early cyclamineus types of narcissus, I have added later blooming jonquils. As I savor the fullness each season has to offer, I think of my mother's advice whenever I gobbled my food as a child. "Slow down," she told me. "Enjoy it!"

This late April view, looking over the formal hellebore bed to the hillside, shows how the sections of the garden play off and with each other, and how the entire garden works together to create a symphony of color and texture.

Perennials, like this selection of my 'Brandywine Hybrid' hellebores, provide a variety of interest throughout the year. Hellebores, in particular, provide unsurpassable color when in bloom in winter and early spring and a bold evergreen foliage texture throughout the year.

THE ROLE OF PERENNIALS

Because we want the promise of seeing something different each time we walk out the door, we use a predominance of ever-changing and often ephemeral herbaceous perennials in the garden at Brandywine Cottage. Annuals, especially modern hybrids, are bred to bloom nonstop from the time you pop them out of their cell packs in April until the plants finally turn to mush the morning after the first hard frost. Such plants are perfect for anyone who wants to plant their gardens or containers just once a year. But for me, a bed with only annuals is too static, providing color and texture but never changing, just more of the same for months on end.

Herbaceous perennials are all about change. From bare ground, these plants emerge in the spring, foliage unfurling and often changing shape and color as it matures, flower stalks extending, buds forming, blossoms opening. Each of these stages of growth can be used in various layers throughout the year—the early foliage providing one color effect, the flowers adding another, the green leaves providing shape and texture, the berries and dried seed heads adding late-season and winter interest. It is even fair game to use plants in their senescence, as with the dried seed heads of many grasses, and the bright yellow fall foliage of *Amsonia hubrichtii*, which to my eye outshines its subtle spring blooms. We do use annuals as fillers in the garden and in our containers, but we do not use them exclusively in either place. Perennials form the backbone of our beds and provide the bulk of the beauty.

All these layers of plants, viewed in real time and as time passes, make the garden interesting, and provide us with seemingly endless challenges and surprises. Sometimes we plan our combinations and layers, and they work, but serendipity also plays a role, and teaches us what plants we might throw together more purposefully next year. Sometimes the most memorable garden moments are the most fleeting, as when a single leaf, backlit by the sun, is transformed from opaque to a translucent tracery of veins more beautiful than any stained glass. I hate to leave my garden for any length of time because it means I miss these moments, or the more predictable blooms of favorite plants. It is no consolation to remember that I may have seen these same plants in bloom many times before, and that such transcendent moments are out in the garden every day, if we only pay attention.

DESIGNING THE LAYERED GARDEN

In my classes at Longwood Gardens and in my advice to garden design clients, I stress the importance of making a plan, but not necessarily following it to the letter.

If you have a dream for a space, a plan can help solidify that dream and make vague ideas more concrete, but it should not make your ideas as immoveable as concrete. A plan can serve as an outline, but once you make it, put it in a drawer. The only exception might be the hardscape, such as a formal patio, which can sometimes become a weak point in a garden if it is not carefully designed and constructed. But when dealing with plants, it is best to consider a garden as living sculpture—always in flux and, if we learn to pay attention, always teaching us what it wants to become.

A plan made in one particular moment in time and rigidly followed will satisfy neither the gardener's creativity nor the garden's full potential. If clients force me to commit my ideas to paper, I tell them, "This is only an idea, a sketch." I do not want to hear from them a year down the road, when I change my ideas: "But the plan says you were going to put a yucca here!" That is not following the creative impulses of the moment; that is gardening by numbers.

I have similar advice when it comes to rules. Some gardeners get so hung up on all the "rules" that have been laid down by so many "experts" that they are constantly wondering, "What am I doing wrong?" My first rule for designing a garden is that there are no rules, at least none that everyone must follow. In any creative endeavor, rules help to show us what has worked before, but as we gain more experience, the rules can be put in the same drawer as our plans. You might even find that knowingly breaking the rules can be fun, once you realize that the taste police are not going to knock on the door and drag you away for doing this. The only

My first attempt at designing the north border **(inset)** was not offensive, it was something worse: dull. Twenty years later, you can see the difference, in color choices and other aesthetic characteristics.

CULTIVATING A SENSE OF PLACE

We have much to learn from other gardens and gardening styles. In these days of instant travel and shopping via TV and the Internet, there is no reason for any of us to garden in isolation. But we do not always have to look across the ocean for our influences. After three centuries of ornamental gardening on this continent, I think that American horticulture has come into its own and is something we should celebrate. And it may be stating the obvious, but since the light, soils, and climate vary widely all over the country, I am a firm believer that no single style is appropriate for all the regions of the United States.

I have gotten many ideas from gardens and gardeners around the world, as well as many plants. But I have taken only the plants that I think will thrive in my area, and I have tried to jigger the ideas to fit the particular conditions I have at home. I love Japanese gardens, and have created an area of my garden that emulates the peaceful preciseness of those spaces in a somewhat looser manner. I love English flower borders, and have a number of beds in that style, but if I had tried to recreate those borders plant by plant, I would have ended up with wheelbarrows full of dead plants. My garden may be a melting pot, but in the end I have tried to create an American garden that both reflects and is sensitive to the countryside in the mid-Atlantic region and the simple eighteenth-century farmhouse that it surrounds.

I wanted to make a garden where I could indulge my passion for plants and also celebrate where I lived, in a 1790s Pennsylvania farmhouse.

punishment might be a few raised eyebrows from the primly rule-bound, but these reactions alone sometimes make rule-breaking worthwhile. As in any pursuit, stretching and bending and breaking rules can get out of control. But it is within that tension that gardeners (and any artists) do their work—trying to maintain the balance between too light a touch and being ham-handed, the straight lines and the playfulness.

The bottom line is that a garden should be fun. If plants and gardening are things you are obsessed with, as I am, having fun certainly helps pass all the hours devoted to them. Why spend all this time if we are only following someone else's rules? Experiment, play with colors, do what pleases you, and do not be afraid to change things if you wish. In your own garden, you are the director; you have the ultimate say. Of course, there is much to learn from other gardens and gardeners, from magazines and TV shows and, I hope, even from books like this one. But take what you learn and make it your own. I have run with that idea for more than twenty years, and I plan to continue.

There have been so many "rules" about color in gardening—which ones go well together and which ones do not, which ones are in and which ones are out—that trying to make sense of them all would make a muddle out of anyone's color sense. Rules about color certainly provide guidance, and even prevent anarchy in some cases, but what does it matter if we have a little anarchy in our gardens? We are not talking about riots in the street. As messy as it might be, the only thing hurt by a riot of color is an oversensitive eye. Making messes just might be an integral part of the creative process: think of all the great cooks who started out making mud pies. They tried to eat them, spit them out, and kept on trying until they got it right. Sometimes the way we learn best is by following our impulses, and then sorting out the resulting messes by ourselves.

One fall when I was still in grammar school, I talked my mother into letting me buy tulip bulbs for our garden. I chose every color they had in the store and planted the bulbs like soldiers marching single file, thinking it would be quite elegant to line the walkway and driveway like that. This was not two dozen tulips—I was doing obsessively large plantings even then—and when they came up the next spring, of course everyone commented on how beautiful they were. I will never know if those people were just being kind to a kid, or if they really did not see what I saw, because even at that young age I knew something was not right. The flowers reminded me of the jumble of candy colors in my Easter basket—great if you are a boy with a sweet tooth, but not so great, I realized, for a garden.

This tulip planting was my first lesson in design, and though I surely could not have put it into words back then, "lack of unity" comes to my mind now. As I recall, the following fall I planted tulips again, and this time they were all one color. They still might have soldiered down the driveway, but eventually I learned that lesson, too—that they would look more natural in clumps and drifts. And today, instead of being daunted by

This page: Combining unusual plants, as in this match between the flower of *Trillium luteum* and the golden leaves of a *Convallaria* cultivar, is more than good design. It makes people think. The most frequent comment I hear about this combination is, "What are those plants?"

Opposite: Taking a cue from the white flowering dogwoods and white color of the cottage, we added the white tulips to bring the color down to ground level in a controlled way.

Repeating colors across borders (here, from the west border of the vegetable garden into the north border) helps unify the garden. In spring, I like to work primarily in pastels, which look particularly pleasing in the angular, pristine light of this season.

tulips (as I might have, if the color police had arrested me after the tulip incident), I plant them all over my garden.

Another childhood memory: Grandmother Culp had a narrow border beside her house in Florida, and one year when I was visiting, I noticed she had planted flowers that were bronzy brown, yellow, orange, and peachy—odd sunset colors. I am certain this combination was not in vogue, but she was following her own vision, and a vision of this richly hued bed stayed with me—perhaps traumatized me—for years. "What a weird lady my grandmother is," I thought. "Nobody else I know uses colors like this in *their* gardens."

Psychologists understand that stimuli from when we are young, like being baffled by a grandmother's color choices, can trigger responses many years later. Now I use these colors in my garden, and where did that idea come from? It did not just pop into my head, and I do not remember reading anywhere that this was trendy. In many cases I do give myself permission to push the limits, buck the trends, break the rules—but maybe in this case I was simply remembering and recreating what my grandmother did so many years ago. A moral of this story might be that there really is nothing new in horticulture, just new gardening grandsons to rediscover everything their grandmothers did.

My one rule about color is that you should do what you like; that way you are assured of pleasing at least one person in this world. Take the rest of what anyone says as guidelines, and let your own eyes be the judge. If you do not like the combinations shown in the pictures in this book, I will not be insulted. And if you do like them, feel free to claim them as your own. I am all about sharing.

When I started this garden, I did not follow this advice. In early years I did not even use any yellow. Less experienced and more impression-able, I had bought into the pinky-blue palette so fashionable back in the 1980s. Fast-forward a few years, and with my confidence ratcheted up a few notches, I realized that this was my garden, to do with as I pleased. If I liked a particular color, no matter how gaudy or outré, then it was my job to make it work. Yes, using some colors can be a challenge. Orange is one, because of its attention-getting brightness—there is a reason that traffic cones, safety vests, and life preservers are this color. But just as there are no bad plants, no color is intrinsically bad. It needs to be con-sidered in context, in juxtaposition with other colors.

I remember attending a lecture at which a well-known gardener stated that you should never use yellow and pink together. This did not sound right to me—I thought immediately of all the pink flowers that have yellow anthers—so I went out in my garden and proved this speaker wrong. I combined pink roses with yellow honeysuckle on the pillars in my rose bed, and pink phlox and yellow black-eyed Susan (*Rudbeckia hirta*) in my border—and both combinations stood up well under the bright midsummer light. The amount of light or shade in which a particular combination is viewed, which also can change with the time of day and

CONVERSATIONS ABOUT COLOR

When Christopher Lloyd, the renowned English plantsman and one of my horticultural heroes, visited my garden, we got into a discussion about "values" (the relative lightness or darkness) of colors. Known to take a point for argument's sake, he insisted that colors in a particular border should all be of the same value. With some trepidation (it was like arguing with the Pope), I dared to disagree, saying different color values, by providing more or less contrast, can give depth or accent or bounce to a particular composition. One example of similar values would be to use the magenta flowers of *Geranium psilostemon* with the acid-yellow *Achillea* 'Coronation Gold'. My point was that a softer yellow yarrow, perhaps *Achillea* 'Moonshine', would make the

color of the geraniums pop even more. Suffice it to say, he was unconvinced.

Graham Stuart Thomas (another Englishman, and another hero) said that strong colors should be used around the house, and softer colors away from the house, to make the garden seem larger as the colors seemed to recede into the background. This does work, but Gertrude Jekyll (you guessed it: English, and my heroine) suggested putting brighter colors at a distance, especially in winter, to catch the eye and draw you out. One way I do this is by placing *Hamamelis* ×*intermedia* varieties on the hillside, where their bright yellow flowers in February make me want to get out into the cold garden and see what is going on.

In this August view of the north border, I have used bright colors and contrasting shades, because the colors have to stand up to the strong, overhead summer light.

the season, has a definite impact on how it may look to your eye. For me, the same pink and yellow combination that looks wonderful in summer might need brighter colored companions in the lower, slanting light of spring or fall, to make it really pop.

One of the joys of a layered garden is that it allows for flexibility, letting me change the predominant colors in a bed several times during the season: white, along with yellow and pastels, in spring; hot colors such as acid yellow, purple, red, and orange in summer; and warm colors such as creamy yellow, apricot, and burgundy in fall. To me, such changes are what make a garden exciting. If my garden were a book, these changes would make me want to keep turning the pages, keep looking.

Color-themed gardens do not need to be all of the same color exclusively. For example, a white garden will look better with blue flowers as an accent, rather than bluish-whites or yellowish whites, which in this context can look dirty or unflattering. Another color accent can enhance the values of the featured color (or provide a contrast, if that is your wish). White heightens the color of any other color it is placed beside. For a different effect, purple, bronze, and some shades of gray soften any brighter colors next to them. When in doubt, I add blue, which works with both hot colors and cooler pastels.

Many people are initially drawn to gardening by the colors of flowers—I know I was. But over many years of designing with plants, I have come to believe that the shape of plants, more than their colors, is what gives any garden its drama and punch. Try taking a photograph of your garden, edit out the color, and see how interesting this picture is. If you can make out distinct shapes and textures (texture being the surface quality of a shape), then you have probably gotten this right. If everything in your picture seems to blend together, it may be time to invite some bolder plants to your garden party.

My garden's signature shape is provided by upstanding plants and man-made elements with vertical profiles. Since the predominant orientation of the garden is horizontal, these verticals—by piercing that horizontal plane—stand out, connect the earth to the sky, and help carry the eye from space to space when repeated throughout the garden. The rose pillars, bamboo teepees, and even the pointed pickets of the vegetable garden fence provide year-round vertical interest, while our selection of upright plants changes with the seasons. Taking the north border as an example, springtime verticality is provided by the flowers of *Digitalis* species, *Salvia nemorosa* 'Caradonna', and *Stachys macrantha* 'Superba', to name a few; in the summer, specimens of *Kniphofia*, *Acanthus*, and *Thermopsis*; and in fall, *Leonotis*, *Canna*, and *Agastache* selections. In all three seasons, *Phormium* specimens in containers add verticality to the same border.

While some vertical plants end up towering over human beings, the key is not their sheer size but the contrasts among the plants in a specific grouping or bed. On a smaller scale, the strappy, pointed leaves of irises can provide vertical interest after the flowers have bloomed. The same

The trees that cover more than half the property gave me the cue for the use of verticals in the borders. The combinations I like best intermingle interesting shapes and textures as well as colors.

Having a signature shape is as important as having a signature color. I like vertical shapes, for the sense of drama they impart to my garden.

can be said for various ferns poking through a woodland garden composed mostly of groundcovers. Even the flower stalk of bolting lettuce can be a vertical accent in the vegetable garden (at least until Michael cannot stand it anymore and rips it out).

Shapes and textures are especially useful in punching up the interest in a shade garden, where any plants that flower tend to be subtler than their sun-loving counterparts. There is a wealth of shade plants with bold-shaped leaves, like hostas and hellebores, as well as many lacy-leaved plants, such as ferns. The challenge is to find vertical and finer grass-like shapes to add to these combinations. Many species of the shade-loving genus *Carex* fit both these bills, providing grassy texture and upright interest. Natives like *C. pensylvanica*, *C. plantaginea*, and *C. flaccosperma*, make themselves even more useful by thriving in dry situations once they are established. The pleated leaves of *C. plantaginea* can provide added texture to plantings. It is also semievergreen, which extends its season of interest and, as with all evergreen plants, makes it a great foil for ephemeral flowers. Both *C. flaccosperma* and *C. laxiculmis* 'Bunny Blue' offer a glaucous, gray-blue color note that tends to lighten up areas of deep shade, and provide a contrast or complement to other plants in the garden.

Selections of *Hakonechloa macra* offer shade gardeners grassy foliage in a range of bright colors. 'Aureola', with a graceful texture and arching mounded habit, is beautiful as a specimen or in drifts. Both 'Aureomarginata', with its yellow variegation, and 'All Gold' will light up a shady

Opposite: Some people do not like using umbels in their gardens, since many weeds (such as Queen Anne's lace) have flowers of this type, but I like using plants like this *Angelica gigas* for just that natural feeling. They also provide horizontal elements that work well with adjacent verticals. The places where these vertical and horizontal planes intersect are where the excitement happens in a garden.

This page, left: I am not a hosta collector, but I find the genus *Hosta*'s variety of leaf shapes and colors to be important design elements in my shady borders.

Right: I like *Acanthus spinosus* for its unusual vertical flower spikes, and because it does well in dry conditions.

area; these two cultivars work well with other yellow or yellow-variegated shade plants. 'Albovariegata' is a good companion for plants with white or cream variegations. Recent introductions such as 'Nicolas', 'Beni Kaze', and 'Naomi' have green leaves that turn red in fall, offering another color to brighten up the shade. I especially like 'Beni Kaze' (Japanese for *red wind*) because its red coloration appears earlier than the other two. Even the dark green foliage of the straight species, *H. macra*, is compelling, if in a more serene and understated way.

I also love the strappy evergreen (really ever-purple) foliage of *Ophiopogon planiscapus* 'Nigrescens', which seems to mimic the patterns of light and shadow on the forest floor. Every year I find more uses for its deep-purple, near black color, which is an elegant addition to many combinations in the shade. We use many potted *Agave* specimens as accents in the sunny parts of the garden, their spiny leaves arching out from the center like so many synchronized divers leaping from a single point. Selections of *Sempervivum* can be architectural in a similar way, if on a much smaller scale. Other shapes I use throughout the garden include the bubble shape of flowers like alliums, and the chalice shape of hellebores and magnolias. With all these plants, a single specimen will stick out like a sore thumb, so I try to use many specimens, often spread through several beds.

When parts of the garden start to get loose and blowsy in the summer months, I like to beef up this layer by adding cannas and bananas. Anyone who has grown these tropical plants knows that the flowers are secondary; what they provide is the bold shape of their large, glossy leaves and a dramatic upright accent that will carry through until frost cuts them down, by which time they are among the last sentinels in the garden.

Our garden does not have the luxury of distinct areas—separated from each by other walls, hedges, or other visual barriers—which can be as different as night and day. Except for the ruin garden, which was created in the ruins of a stable next to the barn on the property, each of our beds and borders can be viewed from many others, so I have tried to make them all relate to one another even while giving each its own character. My goal has been to create a series of garden rooms without walls in which the transitions between the different areas, rather than feeling abrupt and jarring, meld more or less seamlessly together.

One key to creating unity in a garden full of diversity is repetition. I repeat plants in different beds, sometimes the same plants and other times different species of the same genus. I repeat colors across garden areas, as well as vertical accents and other shapes and textures. Each season can have a predominant color, or a genus that takes center stage, which is an easy way to unify different areas. The straight edges of the borders of our garden are appropriate for the age of the house, but these neat lines also provide continuity and definition to our otherwise ebullient planting style. Another repeating element that ties the various garden areas

together is the paths and walls, which are composed of similarly colored stone and gravel, as well as grass.

As various self-sowing species of *Corydalis*, *Thalictrum*, *Rudbeckia*, *Dicentra*, *Stylophorum*, *Crocus*, and *Chionodoxa* spread themselves throughout the garden, they loosen up the design, naturalize and soften the space, and make the garden look like it has a mind of its own, which, of course, it does. A garden can be akin to theater, but there can also be magic in the air, sleight of hand performed by a gardener who knows how to manipulate plants and point of view. If self-sowing plants make a garden look loose and happy, I try to extend this illusion to make it appear as if other plants are self-sowing as well. One way I do this is with the arrangement of hostas on the hillside. By pairing larger varieties higher up the hill with smaller ones of the same leaf color and form below—*Hosta* 'Big Daddy' with the smaller 'Blue Cadet', 'Sum and Substance' with the diminutive 'Zounds', *H. sieboldiana* with the *H.* 'Mouse Ears' series—it looks as if the larger plants are happily scattering their progeny down the hill. In this and many other ways, I see myself as the wizard behind the curtain, manipulating the scene in thought-provoking but not obvious ways, always trying to let the plants and their natural beauty speak first.

As well versed in the theoretical aspects of design as any of us might be, our ideas eventually have to be interpreted in the context of an actual garden site. We like to think of ourselves as the creators of our gardens, and in many ways this is true. But our gardens also help to make them-

Left: I use *Crocus tommasinianus* not only for its colorful blooms (shown on the hillside in February), but also because it naturalizes freely.

Right: I use many forms of corydalis in my garden, including the soft rose-red *Corydalis solida* 'George Baker' and the yellow-flowered *C. cheilanthifolia*. The latter plant sows itself into crevices of the stone walls. Before it blooms, its foliage is often mistaken for a diminutive fern.

As a collector, I need to use every trick in the book to give the garden unity. Here, the blue of *Myosotis sylvatica* links the beds together. Beware of overplanting forget-me-nots; one small specimen of this biennial can spread to cover a wide territory.

selves by clearly showing us what will and will not thrive in the particular conditions available. Accepting these limitations can take time: How many gardeners have imagined that they have enough light to grow the sun-loving plants they love, only to finally realize, several years and many dead plants down the road, that what they really have is a shade garden? Some frustrated gardeners, faced with the inability to grow what they want, may resort to drastically altering a site to accommodate their desires.

When I moved to Brandywine Cottage, I pretty much left the landscape as I found it, but another gardener might have clear-cut the hillside to get more sun, amended the soil with truckloads of organic matter to make it more moisture-retentive, created a waterfall and dug a pond to house water lilies and a school of colorful koi. While such landscape makeovers can work, they can be very expensive, and by altering the natural landforms they can also lead to unintended consequences. If I had made all of these alterations, chances are that the soil on the hillside would have eroded and the well, which was there and working, would have run dry. At the very least, the simple historic character of the property would have been irrevocably changed, and the wildlife the garden now harbors would have been far less diverse.

Certainly, a successful and beautiful layered garden could have been created here even if the site had been heavily altered. But Michael and I have a general philosophy of gardening that could be summed up by saying that we try to work within our means and leave a light footprint on the land. This philosophy—which extends to our minimal use of watering, fertilization, and pesticides—might seem to have little to do with the layered garden, but in fact it has everything to do with it, since it has informed all of our choices, from the particular plants we choose to the methods by which we grow them.

Rather than trying to force our own wishful thinking onto a piece of ground, I believe we can avoid much wasted time and effort by learning to garden with the site rather than against it. It is what we have tried to do: work with what we found to make a garden that looks inevitable, rather than imposed on the landscape. While this path might seem easier, because it involves no drastic interventions, in some ways it is more challenging because it demands that we carefully observe the site over time so we can learn what it has to offer. A garden might be compared to a favorite book: the more time we spend in it, the more we read between the lines, the more we can glean from it and the more delight we can experience from it. The flaw in this analogy is that authors do not rewrite their books between our readings, while gardens are always being rewritten, either by our own hands or the unseen hands of their original creator— which means we can never stop paying attention.

When I began working on the Brandywine Cottage property in February 1990, I had to spend months cleaning it up before I could even consider making a garden. As I worked my way across the acreage, I

The ruin garden, in the beginning (top) and twenty years later (bottom): I tried to accept the property as I found it, and in the ruined stable, I immediately saw an important piece of hardscape that I wanted to celebrate and work with. The two troughs were only the lead in the novel that the ruin has become.

I like to make color combinations at all levels of the garden. In April, at tree level, the pink flowers of *Prunus* 'Okame' combine with the new chartreuse foliage of a willow.

Top: I found numerous black walnut trees on the property, which were an important food source for early residents but are the bane of anyone trying to garden beneath them because they affect the soil. *Actaea* 'Brunette', with unusual purple stems and foliage, is one of many plants that will tolerate this location.

Bottom: *Sanguinaria canadensis* f. *multiplex* 'Plena', a cultivar of native bloodroot, will also grow under black walnut trees. Something this beautiful would seem difficult to grow, but I have had it in the garden for twenty years. When in bloom, it stops traffic on our garden paths.

began to get a feel for the landscape. For any gardener, giving a new property time to reveal itself keeps us from doing anything that we might have to undo later, and will inform many future planting decisions. I noted how the light played across the property, through the day and over the seasons; where water collected after rainstorms and where the soil dried out first. By watching where the snow melted first, I discovered warmer spots that I knew would be possible locations for late-winter bloomers or borderline hardy plants. If you are going to garden with minimal water and fertilizer, as we do, it also is important to figure out what type of soil you have, and its pH level, before you waste money planting (and losing) a host of inappropriate plants.

In learning the lay of the land, I came to appreciate trees more than I ever had before. As a designer, I knew that mature trees can help a new garden look older and more established, and by providing shade they certainly make it more comfortable, especially in the summer heat. They also provide a layer of interest that most people neglect, with foliage and bark colors and textures that can be echoed and contrasted both in other trees and in the shrub and herbaceous layers below. As a remnant of the forests of the mid-Atlantic region, the native trees also contributed to the garden's sense of place. Native trees and shrubs thrive in their indigenous habitats, so reestablishing them in the garden links the created landscape at Brandywine Cottage to the larger wild garden beyond.

If these were the only reasons I had for leaving most of the trees I found here, I still would have been doing a good thing. But I also knew that trees provide both food and habitat for a wide range of wildlife— birds, squirrels and other mammals, and a host of insects from butterflies to beetles. For those of us with trees on our properties, how we maintain them will determine how much benefit they provide for these other forms of life. Dead trees could be considered unsightly, but we leave them standing on our hillside, where the holes in them provide homes for cavity-nesting animals, and the rotting wood provides food for insects, which in turn become food for other animals like woodpeckers. Neither do we remove all fallen twigs or logs from the hillside; we may move this debris if it lands on a choice plant, but otherwise this material is left, along with the fallen leaves, to break down into the humus that acts as the natural fertilizer of the woodland. We sometimes carefully limb up our trees, to allow more light for the understory plants, but we do this purposefully and not often, since once removed, a limb cannot be superglued back on.

Just as trees give visual definition and interest to a landscape, they also define what we can grow beneath them, by the amount of light they let through their canopies, the shallowness of their roots, the amount of moisture they need and, in some cases, the chemicals they secrete. In inventorying the trees, I identified a small stand of *Juglans nigra*, a native black walnut tree that exudes a chemical called juglone that prevents many other plants from growing beneath it. Someone else might have cut down these trees and planted something more benign, but I took it as my special challenge to find genera that would live in their vicinity. Over the years I have developed a good list— *Aucuba, Smilacina, Asarum, Pulmonaria, Convallaria, Helleborus, Hosta, Disporum, Sanguinaria, Cimicifuga, Galanthus, Tricyrtis*—with which to make interesting combinations and layers in this part of the garden.

On the down side, over time I discovered a number of plants that simply will not grow here. Most moisture-loving plants have a hard time, along with those that need acidic soil, like many members of the Ericaceae. In the South, I had grown to love evergreen azaleas, and when I moved to Brandywine Cottage, I blithely assumed that they were easy to grow. It was difficult for me to accept that many of them liked neither the pH nor the dryness of the soil in my northern garden. Eventually I learned that the deciduous azaleas do much better for me, but I killed a number of plants in the learning process.

This list of failures could be much longer—I have friends who save all the labels of the plants they have killed as a reminder not to try them again—but I would rather not dwell on what dies when there are so many plants that live and so many new ones to try. I believe that any resourceful gardener can come up with a satisfying palette of plants that will thrive on any particular site. For me, some of the plants that thrive here turned out to be ones I already loved, like hellebores (along with many members of their family, Ranunculaceae). Others I tried after seeing them growing well in similar conditions elsewhere, and when they did well here too, I fell in love with them. In Italy, I saw *Arum italicum* thriving on a dry hillside, and I came home, planted it on my own dry hillside, and have loved it ever since. It is good advice, in the garden and beyond, to love what loves us back, and not to covet what loves the gardens of others.

MAINTAINING THE LAYERED GARDEN

For anyone trying to create a garden, layered or not, it is crucial to define the extent to which you will pamper your plants to achieve the look and effects you desire. It makes no sense to plant moisture-lovers unless you have the water to support them, or to plant hybrid tea roses unless you commit to a fertilization and pesticide-application regimen to keep them looking good. Knowing how much time and effort you are willing to devote to maintenance should play a large part in defining both the plants you will grow and the type of garden you will create.

Although Brandywine Cottage abuts a suburban development, it is too far out in the countryside to be connected to a municipal water supply. We rely on a 360-foot-deep, slow-filling well for all our needs, which means that if we are to "garden with the site," we have to keep the water needs of the garden to a minimum. We have a lawn, which we seed every year so it at least has a predominance of grass over other green plants, but

we do not fertilize or water it. It is not only the lawn that gets little pampering here. Unless the weather is blazing hot and dry for days, we hardly water anything at all, and we rarely use chemical fertilizers.

In creating new beds at the garden's inception, I tilled in generous amounts of compost and cow manure to add organic matter to the soil. Each year we top-dress the beds with a thin layer of triple-shredded hardwood mulch or leaf mold—so thin that it must be done every year. The idea is not so much to suppress weeds, since this would also suppress the self-sowing plants we like to encourage, but more to feed the soil. Once or twice we have applied low-nitrogen fertilizer in late winter, but we are careful not to overdo this. Too much fertilizer can make plant stems overly long, weak, and floppy. Also, the more fertilizer you use, the more leaves the plants put out and the more water they require. Even if we had a more generous well, we would still choose to grow our plants "lean and mean," which makes them look more natural, conserves water, and makes the entire garden more sustainable.

A layered garden could be compared with a theatrical production of many acts: a variety of players take center stage at different times. As with stagecraft, the trick is in the timing, making sure that each plant gives up the limelight gracefully to the next plant, and no plants hog the stage or

In late March, it is "all systems go!" for the borders surrounding the vegetable garden. After cutting everything back, putting down a light mulch, and painting the fence if necessary, it is time for us to step back and let the plants perform.

PLANTS THAT TOLERATE DROUGHT

We spent two years photographing the garden for this book. In the first year (2010), we suffered through the second driest summer in twenty years, coupled with several heat waves with many days in a row over 90°F. During the drought, one of my gardening friends provided instructions on her Facebook page on how to do a rain dance. In our desperation, we were even hoping that the latest hurricane or tropical depression would come up the coast—winds be damned, we needed the rain!

By the time the rains finally came back, many of the plants were crisped, and needless to say, the garden looked far from perfect. I walked around the garden in a heat-induced daze, dismayed by all I was seeing—but then I remembered that I am supposed to be an optimist, so I tried viewing the aftermath through a different set of eyes. Looking at the plants objectively, I saw that many had not only survived but still looked good, even if the overall picture had suffered. From this experience, I came up with the following list of some of the plants that did well in our drought. I will be adding more of these plants to the beds, as a form of insurance in case hard, dry times come again.

Native plants, for sun: specimens of *Solidago*, *Rudbeckia*, *Ruellia*, *Symphyotrichum*, *Echinacea*, *Verbesina*, *Ephedra*, as well as *Coreopsis tripteris* and *Sanguisorba canadensis*. For shade: *Actaea pachypoda*, *Carex plantaginea* and *C. pensylvanica*, and *Dryopteris ×australis*.

Non-natives, for sun: specimens of *Salvia* and *Nepeta*, as well as *Calamintha nepetoides*, *Agastache* 'Blue Fortune', *Patrinia scabiosifolia*, *Sedum* 'Matrona', *S.* 'Autumn Joy', *S.* 'Valerie Finnis' and other tall sedums; and *Euphorbia palustris*, *E.* 'Diamond Frost', and other spurges. For shade: specimens of *Cephalotaxus*, *Pulmonaria*, and *Epimedium*, as well as *Trachelospermum jasminoides*, *Ophiopogon planiscapus* 'Nigrescens', *Hydrangea anomala* subsp. *petiolaris*, and *Prunus laurocerasus*.

In general, all succulents did well, especially our collection of agaves, as did many summer bulbs, including gladiola, summer hyacinth, and calla lily. I was also pleased that the foliage of irises and lilies, which I appreciate as a vertical accent long after the flowers are gone, held up well.

The genus *Euphorbia* includes many species and varieties that will not only tolerate periods of drought, but come through it looking good, such as *Euphorbia griffithii* 'Dixter' (left), *Euphorbia palustris* (center), and *Euphorbia dulcis* 'Chameleon' (right).

step on another's toes as they make their entrances and exits. Rather than a comedy of errors (which no gardener wants) or a tragedy (which the weather sometimes forces on us), my goal is to create a sublime horticultural drama, full of surprises that keep the audience engaged.

Creating these surprises and having them play out in a seamless fashion is a never-ending task. Any garden with a succession of plants grown closely together will have places where vigorous plants butt up against less vigorous neighbors. And it is up to the gardener to arbitrate these territorial disputes and do what needs to be done to assure that the weaker plants get enough space and light to thrive. This editing process is not the same as drawing a line in the bed, and snipping off any part of any plant that dares cross into the territory of another. Editing in a garden, especially one in which a naturalistic effect is desired, needs to be more subtle than that. It can be as simple as nipping off a few leaves from a taller plant that is shading a smaller neighbor, or as drastic as the outright removal of extra plants that have self-sown or spread into another's territory.

With herbaceous perennials that die back every year, such editing does no permanent harm. Pruning woody shrubs has to be more carefully thought out, to avoid deforming the shape and structure of the plant. One example in our garden is *Viburnum rhytidophyllum*, which has to be

I much prefer to work with, and thin if necessary, plants that have a vigorous nature than to do extensive horticultural acrobatics to get a plant to grow. I would not want to do without the sky-blue flowers of *Symphytum azureum*, even though I have to rip much of it out every other year to prevent it from overrunning choice plants like my black hellebores.

carefully pruned in order to allow a neighboring variegated *Cornus mas* to grow and express itself.

Other plants we often have to liberate from aggressive neighbors include peonies, irises, epimediums, and kniphofias. With ephemeral plants such as trilliums, *Cardamine quinquefolia*, and *Cypripedium parviflorum* (lady's slipper orchids), as well as many spring bulbs, allowing the foliage to die back naturally without being overshadowed is particularly important, since these plants have only a short window in which to emerge, bloom, and then recharge before going dormant. Sometimes the aggressors are common self-sowing plants that, once removed, end up on the compost pile. But in this collector's garden, even rarities have their run-ins once in a while. I have a hundred-dollar variegated lily of the valley from Japan that keeps trying to overrun a hundred-dollar clump of galanthus. The consolation is that any division I can pry off the lily of the valley (a beautiful plant, variegated in an unusual spatter pattern) makes a nice gift for a friend, or can be traded with other collectors for plants to add to the mix.

Besides editing, in a garden like ours where both gardeners have high standards for neatness and beauty, weeding and grooming are constant tasks. Michael enjoys cutting back and deadheading more than I do, whereas I enjoy weeding more, so we are well matched in the maintenance department. Herbicides are not an option; hand weeding is the norm in our garden. I like weeding because it gets me up close and personal with my plants and gives me a pleasing sense of accomplishment once the job is done. I especially enjoy this work when I return from a trip, because it gets me up to speed with what might have happened in the garden while I was gone.

I do admit that as an imperfect human being I am not a perfect weeder, and this point was made crystal clear by a garden visitor a few years ago. She noticed a plant with a serrated leaf in one corner of the garden that she thought was a poppy, and called me over to help confirm its identity. What I found was no poppy—it was one of the world's largest specimens of *Taraxacum officinale* (dandelion), which I had somehow overlooked in my weeding. As a joke I told her, "It's a dandelion, but the white-flowered form," and we laughed as I made a mental note to dig it out as soon as she left. The real joke was that I was only half-joking. I had once been offered *T. albidum*, the white dandelion from Japan, but in a rare moment of restraint I turned it down.

Long ago I decided I could tolerate a garden that had a few chewed leaves because I would never want a garden without all the living things I love—the birds, bees, butterflies, fireflies, ladybugs, and so many more that might be harmed if I used chemicals to kill the leaf-munching critters. Like the preceding roundabout sentence, life is a circle: everything is interconnected and no one thing can be removed from a system without upsetting the balance. I could add fungi to the list of things I tolerate, like black spot on my roses. I would rather come up with a way to hide the

These diminutive garden performers can live in our garden because we almost never use chemical pesticides. Each of these insects is doing something besides providing us with momentary visual pleasure: **(A)** the praying mantis egg case will hatch out a host of insect-eaters; **(B)** the ladybugs on the *Asclepias* specimen are eating aphids; **(C)** the bee is pollinating *Stachys officinalis*; **(D)** and the black swallowtail larva will eventually metamorphose into a fluttering garden diva. **(E)** Monarch butterflies always add an otherworldly effect to the garden when they stop over on their late summer migration. **(F)** The "writing spider" (*Argiope aurantia*) inspires awe because of its size and color, and its unique ornamental web.

COPING WITH DEER

For most animals our hospitality is open-armed, but there are some uninvited guests that we would rather not have eating at our garden table. Deer are the least welcome. For now, we have no fence around the property (because of both the unattractiveness of such a structure, and the expense), so we rely on repellents to keep the depredations of these critters to a minimum. These liquid repellents are based on some form of animal protein, making the deer think there is a predator in the area and so they stay away.

Deer are mostly a problem in our garden in late winter and early spring, when they are foraging widely for anything remotely edible. At those times of year, I spray repellents on the hillside and other parts of the property at least once every two weeks, and more often if the season is particularly rainy. Snowy weather also makes the deer more desperate by covering up many sources of food. The trick is to get the deer to think that predators live in the garden, so I change the repellents often to keep them from growing accustomed to any one of them. I begin spraying early, in January, and need to remain vigilant, or else. One year I grew complacent and lost five good-sized camellias overnight. In other seasons, I watch for signs of deer browsing (often on my lilies) and spot treat those plants, which usually works to deter nibbling deer.

When it comes to deer and bulbs, the rule of thumb used to be that they dislike members of the Amaryllidaceae but love those in the Liliaceae. This was before house-wrecking botanists split up these families and made a hash of this simple, if silly rule. What I can now say for certain is that deer do not favor narcissus and galanthus (both still in the Amaryllidaceae) and will feast on lilies and tulips (still in the Liliaceae). As for the rest, I will not go on the record—the safest route to take when predicting the appetites of deer, which seem to get less picky and more goat-like in their taste as time goes by.

disfigurement (in this case, by growing other plants to hide the denuded canes) than spray a fungicide that might kill more than just the fungus spores.

Another fungus, powdery mildew, often disfigures the leaves of herbaceous perennials, with phlox and monarda being among the most susceptible. In my garden I now have a pink-flowered strain of *Phlox paniculata* that has the mildew-resistant cultivar 'David' as one of its parents. By continuing to rogue out any mildewed plants before they go to seed, I hope to increase the resistance of this strain as the years go by. Trials in the 1990s at the Chicago Botanic Garden and elsewhere identified resistant varieties of *Monarda*; I grow one called 'Jacob Cline' that looks good most years. Some years it does not—resistance is no guarantee against disease, but only gives the plants a better chance—and there are few sadder sights in a garden than a flower struggling to bloom atop a three-foot stalk of mildewed, dying foliage. If this is how monarda grew in colonial times, no wonder gardeners stripped all the leaves and brewed them into Oswego tea (another common name for the plant).

As breeders have proven with these and other plants, it is possible to select varieties for their disease resistance and not just for the newest flower color or leaf variegation. In Germany, laws prohibiting the application of chemical pesticides on plants in public spaces have created a larger market for disease-resistant varieties. As consumers we have to demand this, not only to make our gardens easier to maintain, but for the sake of our lives, and all the lives that share the garden with us.

Where the pest is an insect, like a Japanese beetle, Michael and I handpick them whenever we can. Having insectivorous mobile garden art, which is how I sometimes view my chickens, also helps keep insect populations down, though if we are not careful to protect them, the chickens can be carried off by four-legged or avian predators and become part of the food chain themselves.

Beyond the harm to local wildlife, any chemicals we used in our garden might end up polluting our well, or run off the property. In a heavy rainstorm, this runoff may end up in nearby Beaver Creek, a tributary to the Brandywine Creek, which runs into the Delaware River, which flows into the Atlantic Ocean. These kinds of direct connections with the outside world exist in every garden, which is why I think we should always aim, in our gardening practices, to do the least harm and the greatest good.

CHAPTER TWO

The GARDEN at BRANDYWINE COTTAGE

TO GIVE YOU A SENSE OF HOW A LAYERED GARDEN works, this chapter takes you on a tour of Brandywine Cottage, starting at the outermost edges and moving to the major garden sections, roughly in the order they were completed. The words and pictures describe how Michael and I have created a space that pleases us. But each of us has a different vision of the ideal garden, and ultimately every gardener has to ask himself or herself these questions: What do I want from my garden? What really excites me? What do I think is beautiful? And how much work do I want to do to keep it that way?

THE SCREEN PLANTINGS

The property had once been the heart of an 80-acre farm, the remnants of which had been subdivided by the previous owners into 2-acre lots. When I bought the place, I knew that twenty new houses were going to be built behind and above me, so creating a screen between me and this development was an immediate priority. I wanted Brandywine Cottage to be a romantic place where I could forget that I lived in a larger world, a goal that would be impossible if every vista revealed a group of late twentieth-century houses called Brandywine Hunt.

For any gardener, screening out unwanted views is a key to creating privacy and an appropriate mood. Some screens can be ornamental plantings, such as hedges or mixed borders of shrubs and trees, but a screen at its most basic can be a simple wooden fence. The idea is to create a backdrop that at best may complement but in no way competes with the garden's plantings and design. The utility of a screen is most apparent where one is lacking: a garden can be filled with the most beautiful plants on earth, but if the backdrop is a string of cars parked in the neighbor's driveway or a woodpile covered with a bright-blue tarp, the eye will instead focus on those unattractive distractions.

The hillside and its tree canopy served as a natural screen to the north of the garden, and to the south and on the road side, a wooden fence would do the job well. The problem was on the east, where the neighboring property had been raised up by the developer and a new house was built that loomed over my garden like a castle in the air. No normal-sized fence would hide this house, so evergreen trees were the only solution. The previous owner had begun by planting a row of spruce trees, which I supplemented my first year in the house by planting four white pines about 20 feet in back of the spruces. I added to that back row a mixed border of fast-growing evergreens, including ×Cupressocyparis leylandii and Thuja 'Green Giant', an arborvitae cultivar that stands up much better than other varieties under the weight of heavy snowfalls. Both are also supposed to be deer-resistant, although the jury is still out on that question.

It took about ten years, but this screen eventually filled in, and even though the house and its pool sit only about 75 feet from my back property line, they are no longer visible. This double row of evergreens also serves a secondary screening function. Between them, and mostly hidden from the garden, is a nursery area with holding beds for my hellebore seedlings and other plants, a garden shed, a potting area, and my compost pile.

Other groupings of trees placed in carefully chosen locations on the hillside were planted to help screen out other unwanted views and provide more of the vertical accents I love. A few of these trees were planted years ago when I was laid low by a serious illness and my dear friend Dennis West came to live with us for several months, to help nurse me back to health.

Previous: The path to a layered garden has many twists and turns. Behind the barn, this sheltered nook in the shade of a *Halesia* specimen is a perfect spot to dream about things to come.

Opposite: The stockade fence on two sides of the property has weathered and now blends in with its surroundings. Screens like this, whether living or man-made, also provide protection from the outside world.

A screen can be a row of evergreens, as shown in the background of this view. But design elements, like the white fence and white shed, can provide another kind of screen. Before the trees grew big, the structures helped lead the eye away from the house that loomed over the east side of the property.

Mixed plantings in the fire pit corner of the garden screen an unwanted view and serve as a
transition to the wilder parts of the garden.

I have a line that I use perhaps too often but which is absolutely true: what always keeps me going is that I want to see one more plant bloom and have one more combination to make. This was never more true than when I was recovering from that illness. The whole time I was in the hospital, I thought about getting back into the garden. When I first returned home, I could barely walk a few steps at a time, and the most I could do was sit on the porch and relish the garden's delights. As I grew stronger, Michael or Dennis would put a chair in the ruin garden, where I could sit in the sun and weed my troughs. Later I was able to sit along the walls at the bottom of the hillside and weed, enjoying the beauty and feeling the strength of the garden flow through me, much as a bud must feel the power of rising sap.

Part of my revenge against that health incident was to live my life as normally as possible, as if I had not nearly died. One day in June of that year, when I was still not fully recovered, I decided that I just had to have three specimens of *Juniperus virginiana* in a group on the hillside. As I told Michael and Dennis, who were more than a little dubious, these trees would help fill out the screen I had been creating, and being natives they would look as if they had always been there.

As usual, I wanted instant gratification. No green bananas for me; they had to be big trees, to have immediate impact. But the oversized burlap-covered root-balls were much too large for Michael and Dennis to easily move. Even though I was too weak to offer any physical assistance, I still insisted on micromanaging the planting: "A little to the left please; no, a little to the right." But they could barely hear me over all their grunting and struggling and cursing. They finally got two trees placed, but the third tree had other ideas, and as we walked down the hill to examine our work, it rolled down and nearly bowled us all over.

With that near-miss we decided to call it a day, and to celebrate a job well done (well, really only two-thirds done) we began our cocktail hour a bit early that afternoon. The next day they finished the job, planting the errant red cedar, and now when I look up at that corner of the hillside, instead of being annoyed by a view of the houses of the adjacent development, I see the big trees, think of Michael and Dennis, and smile.

AROUND THE HOUSE

When I first started gardening at Brandywine Cottage, besides working on the planted screen, I began planting the areas closest to the house, something I would suggest for any new homeowner. These are the areas I would see most often, and successes there would cheer me on as I expanded the garden outward. I wanted these beds to feature early blooming plants, so when I dashed in and out in cold weather, I would still get to see something in bloom. Such a design also allows me to view these flowers from the comfort of the house. I should mention that, except for the guest bedroom (where my mother insisted on her privacy), our house has no curtains, so all our windows serve as rectangular picture frames for the ever-changing views outside.

The Jewel Box

The jewel box, a bed between the north side of the house and the driveway, was the first area on the property I planned and planted. I call this garden the jewel box because it houses a number of horticultural treasures, and comprises many jewel-like colors. The original owner had built the beginnings of a rough wall to raise the driveway, which gave me the opportunity to make a series of terraced beds leading from the hillside, across the driveway, and down to the front door of the house. The terrace walls are dry-laid (without mortar) and made of rubble stone that I found on the property and elsewhere nearby, including on construction sites in the neighboring development. I amended the soil in the beds behind the walls with sand and compost because I knew the plants would need better drainage than the original soil would afford. I rarely amend the soil in this way, but when I do, I think it best to amend an entire bed at a time, rather than doing it piecemeal for single planting holes. Such holes can upset a bed's drainage and sometimes become water-retaining "bathtubs" that can drown the plants.

The path through this area follows one that had already been worn by human and dog traffic. It accommodates two people walking side by side, which I consider the minimum width for a functional path. Originally laid with gravel, sand, and some soil compressed with a tamper, we still top-dress it with fresh gravel every few years; I try to match the gravel color as closely as possible to the stone used in the walls.

Seeds love to germinate in this path (and in other similar areas, such as the driveway gravel garden). It takes some effort to remove the weeds and thin the desirable plants that pop up, but if this chore is ignored, these areas can quickly become overgrown. For this reason, some gardeners do not encourage such volunteers, but to me these cheerful self-sowers—including *Galanthus elwesii*, *Dicentra cucullaria*, and *Scilla hispanica*—make the garden look looser and more natural. Since the path is in a low spot that accumulates water during rainstorms, I have also planted various primroses here, which like moister soil than I have in most areas of the garden. I cannot decide which I love more, the plants themselves, with their subtle differences in flower color and form, or the pleasure of leading garden visitors down the primrose path.

The bed itself is banked into the hillside, and seen from the kitchen window it is almost at eye level. From that viewpoint, one has the feeling of looking into a terrarium, or into a jewel box at a collection of little gems. This garden transitions into a shade garden beneath three dogwoods that were growing here when I bought the place, and which

This page: This section of the jewel box is golden in the spring, with *Trillium luteum* and a golden-leaved lily of the valley in the foreground, and a *Dicentra spectabilis* 'Gold Heart' in the background. This is the view from my kitchen window.

Opposite: A "primrose path" through the jewel box connects the house to the rest of the garden. Bordering the path are both treasures and self-sowers—and, of course, primroses.

JEWEL BOX LAYERS

Being close to the house and on the main path leading to the garden, the jewel box garden holds my interest twelve months of the year, with flowers or foliage or bark or all three, depending on the season. In the late winter and springtime, snowdrops, double hellebores, trilliums, Siberian squill (*Scilla species*), dogtooth violets (*Erythronium species*), and other treasures, which might be lost in other areas of the garden, are easy to see and appreciate in this location. Select tender plants—including coleus, a *Cordyline* specimen, and a chartreuse-leaved Boston fern, *Nephrolepis exaltata* 'Rita's Gold'—provide more color once the spring flowers are finished. *Cornus sanguinea* 'Midwinter Fire', a deciduous shrub in the dogwood family, is planted along both sides of the path, and its amber-colored twigs in winter look stunning against the backdrop of the white house. I underplant these shrubs with complementary apricot- and yellow-flowered hellebores, and for year-round interest I have used black mondo grass as well as two variegated aucubas. Container plantings in this bed are changed six times a year, and provide color and interest in all seasons.

Three views of the jewel box from the main borders, in early April (**previous page, top**), two weeks later in April (**bottom**), and in late September (**above**). *Cornus sanguinea* 'Midwinter Fire' is featured in all three views; it is one of our first woody plants to show color in the fall. The evergreen *Aucuba japonica* and the tracery of the *Hydrangea petiolaris* branches on the barn wall also provide winter interest.

inspired me to plant more dogwoods on the hillside nearby. The white dogwoods and the white house gave me the cue for the white phase the garden goes through at tulip time, when we plant masses of lily-flowered *Tulipa* 'White Triumphator' in the main borders. Woodland treasures ornament this shady area, including a scattering of unusual color forms of hellebores and fall and winter flowering cyclamens. Also featured are the native yellow-flowered *Cypripedium*, the golden-leaved *Disporum* 'Dancing Geisha' (which I brought back from Japan), yellow-flowered *Trillium luteum*, a golden-leaved *Convallaria*, and *Dicentra spectabilis* 'Gold Heart'— gold being a common denominator for a jewel box.

The Entry Garden

The entry garden is dominated by four large spruce trees that loom over the house, almost hiding it from the road and making the front door seem like the passage into a Hobbit house. What we call the front door, on the west side of the house, was originally a side entrance. The original front door faced south, toward the road. Now, instead of walking *up* to the front door, as earlier owners would have done, we follow stone steps from the driveway *down* to it. I love entering the garden this way, leaving my car and the real world behind, stepping down into the garden's embrace as it welcomes me home.

The steps are the main path down from the driveway to the house. The original well is used both to stage potted plants and to celebrate the various seasons. The front door to the house is to the right.

Early on I tried to grow grass in this area, which was certainly not "gardening with the site." The spruces are shallow rooted, making the area beneath them dry shade, and I never got more than a wispy carpet to survive. On a subsequent trip to Japan, I fell in love with the gardens and landscapes there, and realized such a style would be perfect for this space. I gave up on grass and moved to plants that like dry shade, as the space had already dictated to me. I emphasized the peaceful, Zen-like feel of this area, spreading pea gravel around the surface roots and placing rocks in the surrounding beds as naturalistic features. My obsessive gardening of this space is also in the Japanese tradition. Because we pass through here many times a day, I try to maintain it more meticulously than other parts of the garden, picking up every stick, raking the gravel, and sweeping off the roots to expose their gnarly forms.

Epimedium and *Trillium* specimens provide color in the spring, in this area and all along the shade border on the south side of the property. Other early bloomers include snowdrops, a few hellebores, and several unusual *Hepatica* selections. After spring blooms fade, this area is mostly one of foliage and textural interest. Dwarf cherry laurels, several deciduous azaleas, and two *Skimmia japonica* are augmented with a selection of ferns, including *Polystichum acrostichoides*, and species and varieties of *Dryopteris*, *Athyrium*, and *Osmunda*. *Hosta* 'Blue Cadet', several varieties of *Aruncus*, and the native *Carex pensylvanica* also thrive in this shady area, the latter looking so much like a mop head of green hair that I am often tempted to comb it.

One plant growing in this area that predated my arrival was *Convallaria majalis* var. *rosea*. This light pink lily of the valley did well here but it seemed lonely, so I sought out other family members to keep it company. I now grow seven *Convallaria* varieties, all of which I love for their fragrance and the fact that they bloom in May, my birthday month.

The original well for the house, which is about 30 feet deep and still functional, is another feature in this garden. I feel lucky to have the real thing and not a "wishing well," though I have used the well to make many requests—my most frequent being, "More rain, please!" The well, with its diminutive shingled roof, is an ideal staging area for shade-loving potted plants.

At some point before I bought the house, an overhanging wood-shingled roof was added above the entry. Soon after purchasing the cottage, I realized that the roof was somewhat decrepit and would have to be replaced, so I planted a garden up there. One of my mottos is, "Give me a place and I'll give you a plant," and the rotting shingles were a great medium for *Opuntia*, a hardy cactus; several varieties of low-growing *Sedum* and *Sempervivum*; *Dicentra formosa*, which self-sowed on the roof; and *Iris tectorum*, the Japanese roof iris. I was on the roof when I first met some of my neighbors, who asked what I was doing. "Putting in a garden," I told them; and if they thought that I was a bit daft at the time, they have become good friends nonetheless.

Beneath an old cedar sits my simple version of an "auricula theater" (a kind of structure built to showcase collections, popular in eighteenth- and nineteenth-century Europe), which I first fell in love with in England. In the spring it houses my collection of *Primula auricula* varieties; in this July view it presents a collection of begonias.

One of the hardest things for me to do was create an outdoor entertaining space that fits with the house and the rest of the garden. The gravel on the patio ties it in with the entry garden around the corner of the house. The table is custom-made from cedar, to echo the red cedars in the space. The peaked roof of the chicken chalet is in the background.

I replaced the shingles about six years ago and this green roof went with them, but before that I remember answering a phone call one morning from a friend in Texas. In the course of the conversation, I told her I was looking out my bedroom window at the roof in bloom. She paused, her disbelief perceptible over a thousand miles of telephone line, and asked me: "David, what time do you take cocktails now?"

The Driveway Gravel Garden

The same obsessive mentality that leads a gardener to plant his roof may sooner or later lead him to plant the driveway. I knew that the gravel in the driveway would be hospitable for a variety of plants, and that we really did not need this bit of a dogleg for parking cars anyway. So now the corner of the driveway just above the jewel box bed is a car-free gathering area and gravel garden, serving as an entry feature at the top of the stone steps leading down to the house.

I took a cue for this area from the English gardener Beth Chatto, whose garden I have visited and whose book, *The Dry Garden*, is one of the best on this subject. Hundreds of species of tulips are planted in the driveway gravel, looking as if they were self-sown. The squirrels and moles and voles find it as hard to dig in the gravel as we do, and do not bother these bulbs like they would if they were planted in regular garden soil. A similar naturalizing effect is created with *Allium karataviense*. I have large oval pots packed full of this allium, surrounded by fifty or more plants growing directly in the gravel. When visitors invariably comment on how happy the plants are to be self-sowing, I smile and tell them my secret: that I planted every bulb in the gravel. To confuse people even more, true self-sowers grow here as well. I count on *Helleborus foetidus* for its green early spring flowers and year-round foliage interest. *Corydalis lutea* starts blooming in spring, takes a break in hot summer months, and reblooms in the fall. I rip out this yellow corydalis when it spreads too far, as I do with the yellow-flowered and mat-forming *Sedum acre* 'Aureum', but both always come back. *Papaver* 'Lauren's Grape', a purple poppy, blooms at the end of May; and *Calamintha nepetoides* and *Silybum marianum* are self-sowing summer features. Around the edge of the bed, I have placed several antique stone troughs and color pots for seasonal interest, and by fall they become the main focus in this bed. We plant pots of colorful plants for seasonal accents and plant displays, changing them seasonally and sometimes more often, which gives another layer to the garden as well as another place to experiment with color.

It is not winter cold that kills *Primula auricula*, but summer heat, and I move my plants to a shadier, cooler garden location in hot weather. I love these plants for their stylized blossoms, and I love being part of a centuries-old tradition of growing them.

The driveway gravel garden is a gathering place for plants and people. All plants here have to survive very dry conditions. The troughs here and in the ruin garden give another element of design unity.

Opposite: I allow plants to self-sow here and I also plant them in the gravel myself. The tulips and alliums were all placed to look as if they had self-sown.

This page, top: The gravel deters the grabby paws of squirrels and chipmunks, who would dig up my *Tulipa* 'Little Princess' in looser garden soil. These small gems, surrounded by gravel instead of other plants, also stand out more here than they would in the crowded garden beds.

Bottom: The short, spritely *Allium karataviense* works perfectly in this space, which also is home to other rock garden plants. This allium is also used in color pots at the same time of year.

The Ruin Garden

Beyond the entry garden is a barn that provides shelter to many tender plants and our chickens in cold weather. Attached to that structure are two remaining stone walls of a stable, the roof of which had caved in by the time I arrived on the scene. Such a tumbledown eyesore, front and center by the road, might have been a problem for some homebuyers. A more sensible person might have torn the structure down completely and started over, but where others saw a lemon, I saw an ice-cold pitcher of lemonade—no, make that a pitcher of margaritas. The remaining walls were basically solid; all I had to do was clean it up, plant the space, and I would have a romantic ruin that many gardeners would kill for. But before the romance could begin, I had to pull off miles of English ivy from the walls and cart away loads of junk.

As in other areas on the property, the space dictated what type of garden we would make here. Any plants we used would have to thrive in full sun, be drought-tolerant, and also tolerate low-pH (or alkaline) conditions, caused by lime leaching from the mortared walls and cement floor. With some experimentation, we found many plants that do well in this garden. We also have a collection of planted troughs that go perfectly with the stone walls of the space.

The ruin is the only space in the garden that is visually separated—being literally walled off—from the others, so I felt freer to make it a bit more eccentric. At first I wondered if a space this odd should be so close to the road, since it serves as a calling card for the garden and its gardeners. But this is where my ruin was—not up on the hillside, where I might have placed it had I been given the choice (and the money)—so this is where I had to make it. On a positive note, it does serve to introduce visitors to the idea that my garden is full of many different plants used in a variety of ways.

Gardens are usually made in the ground, so the most exciting feature of this space, for visitors and for me as a gardener, is how the vertical walls are covered with plants. I started planting in existing crevices where the mortar had dislodged. But these spaces were often not large or numerous enough, so I began deliberately loosening other stones (like a child jiggling a loose tooth) until they fell out. Who knows how far I would have proceeded if a visiting friend had not witnessed me in action and exclaimed, "David, if you pull one more stone out of that wall, it's going to fall down!"

We pushed the ruin's ruination in another way, with Michael delighting in taking a sledgehammer to the concrete floor. He worked at points where cracks had already formed, creating new pockets for plants and softening the space by breaking up the rigid lines of the walls and the rectangular troughs. The passage of time probably could have accomplished this destruction on its own, but we managed to hurry the work along by at least a hundred years.

This May view of the ruin garden features *Tulipa linifolia* 'Bright Gem', the late-blooming *Narcissus* 'Sun Disc', and *Tradescantia* 'Sweet Kate'. *Euphorbia cyparissias*, a weedy spurge that keeps the bulb-eating rodents out of my tulips, also happens to be the right color. All these yellows play off the flowers of the *Corylopsis* specimen in the background.

For anyone driving up the road looking for my garden, this scene lets them know that they have arrived. It also sets the stage for what will be found in the rest of the garden—beautiful combinations of unusual plants, with hardly a space left unplanted.

RUIN GARDEN LAYERS

The layers in the ruin are generally color-based, with the hues of the plants in the wall and floor reflected in the troughs and containers. In early spring, the predominant color is yellow—the flowers of *Corydalis cheilanthifolia*, the new foliage of various dwarf conifers in the troughs, and various color pots containing, among other plants, *Cornus sericea*. The yellows give way to a pink-gray scheme, highlighted by the bloom of *Saponaria ocymoides* that blankets the walls. By the time the soapwort fades, the blues have overtaken this garden, like *Campanula portenschlagiana*, and *Nepeta* species along with brighter accents such as pots of yellow *Phormium* specimens and the white button flowers of *Tanacetum niveum*.

By summer the garden has a Mediterranean feeling, with our collection of agaves and other succulents basking in the heat, and various pots of tender plants like *Lavandula stoechas* and lacy-leaved *Agastache* selections in full bloom. The nepeta in the wall reblooms in late summer, adding another shot of blue to the mix, and in fall, we put in containers of heirloom chrysanthemum varieties. Winter color comes from the dwarf conifers, with pots of yellow-twig dogwood and, depending on my mood, perhaps cut branches of *Ilex verticillata* tucked in here and there, like in a flower arrangement.

This page: An early shot of the ruin area and barn when I first acquired the property. This sight is an all too familiar one in many landscapes: a place right by the road, for all to see, that simply needs somebody to love it.

Opposite: When it is hot and dry, as in this August view, plants like agaves, furcraeas, phormiums, and echeverias strut their stuff. All can survive with minimal water, making them perfect for a guilt-free vacation.

The most fun I had in the early years of creating the garden was planting the walls of the ruin. I felt like Jackson Pollock, throwing colorful plants instead of paint at the wall. If I lived in a city and only had this much space, I would be content with a garden like this.

I planted the wall with small plants, tucking them into the cracks in early spring to help them become established before the baking hot weather arrived—a practice I still follow when I occasionally need to replant. I used plants that are common and easy to grow: clump-forming sempervivums and self-sowers that only need to be edited (weeded out) occasionally. These plants form the backbone in this challenging space, with little treasures rewarding those who take a closer look, including: *Corydalis solida*, a spring bulb that comes in several different color forms; *Saxifraga*, a rock garden genus, some pretty in flower and the encrusted varieties (with powdery white on the leaf edges) beautiful for their foliage alone; the brightly colored flowers of *Lewisia*, surprisingly hardy when given good drainage; and edelweiss (*Leontopodium alpinum*), which anyone of German descent or who likes *The Sound of Music* (I qualify on both counts) has to grow. I also grow dwarf bearded iris here, the leaves of which add a diminutive vertical element. Because this space is protected and south facing, the plants are early to bloom, and also I can grow plants that would not otherwise be hardy in zone 6.

A deck off the second story of the barn, crowded with many potted plants including our collection of *Eucomis* species, covers about a third of the space of the ruin. I enjoy looking down at the ruin garden from this deck, which affords a different perspective, but the transition between the full sun of the walled area and the shade beneath the deck was awkward at first. To smooth this transition, we built a raised alpine bed just under the deck to define and separate the light requirements of the plants below. And we added a utilitarian touch to the scene by nestling in the shade plants behind the alpine bed an old sharpening wheel that looks like it could have been abandoned there by a previous owner.

All the garden surfaces in the ruin are mulched with pea gravel, which ties in with the stone of the walls and the troughs, and helps unify the space with the nearby entry garden, also mulched with gravel. The addition of gravel is a good botanical practice because it improves drainage, keeping moisture away from the crowns of the plants. Many trough and rock garden plants require good drainage to survive, since it is not always the cold but often the winter wet that does a plant in.

We were so pleased with the ruin that we later extended this dry palette of plants into a narrow bed along the roadside to the south of it. The effect now is one of abundance—the plants seem to be spilling out of the ruin and running down the edge of road. Repeating the same plants, including agaves in pots, contributes to the illusion that this roadside bed just happened on its own.

Opposite, top: Individual combinations are not forgotten in the ruin, as in this container with hellebores, a gold-leaf variety of *Acorus gramineus*, pansies, and *Euphorbia* ×*martinii*.

Bottom, left: I made this roadside bed near the ruin before the township highway department erected the sign with the directional arrow. After it went up, I decided to use more yellow in the bed to make the sign look like part of a purposeful combination. In this dry bed, I let plants like *Euphorbia cyparissias* and *Humulus lupulus* 'Aureus' run more than I would in other parts of the garden; they help cover the ground and the fence. This photo was taken in the spring.

Bottom, right: The roadside bed is an extension of the ruin garden, so I used plants here that relate to the plants used in that area. In this mid-July view, the spurge is finished blooming and has become a carpet of green.

Troughs

In more than twenty years of gardening in troughs, I have found that I can grow more interesting plants per square inch in these specialized containers than anywhere else. I started out with two troughs, but over the years I have learned that one or two of anything looks timid and tentative. I now have twenty-seven, roughly half of which can be found in the ruin in any particular year. If something works for me—whether a genus or a color or a trough—my theory is that more is always better. The troughs are a variety of sizes, with some made of solid stone and others of hypertufa—a combination of peat moss, Portland cement, and perlite that can be molded into an infinite number of shapes and looks like stone.

Troughs allow me to tailor the soil, pH, and drainage to best suit plants that need very specific environments. Most are diminutive specimens from alpine regions, less than 12 inches high, which would not survive in my garden beds. Even if they could grow in my beds, they would be much harder to appreciate among larger and more vigorous competitors. Troughs are like miniature raised beds; at their best, they resemble miniature landscapes, in which mountainside flowers find a hospitable home in my Pennsylvania garden. I am not forgetting they are a fitting ornament for this old farmhouse, stone watering troughs having been used by the animals that once lived here.

A soil mix that allows water to drain freely and oxygen to reach the roots is one key to successful trough culture. My mix includes coarse turkey or chicken grit (available at your local feed store), coarse sand, and sterile soil. The ratio is roughly a third of each by volume, but this can be varied to better duplicate the conditions of each plant's native environment. Shade plants, for example, appreciate a mix with a higher percentage of soil. In troughs with more than one type of plant, I make sure that they are all compatible with the particular soil mix I am providing.

Using bagged sterilized or potting soil is better than using garden soil, since the soil should be free of weed seeds and should help prevent fungal problems until the plants become established. I favor potting soil without perlite (Metro-Mix 510, if available, is ideal). Perlite tends to float to the top of a container when watering, which looks unsightly and unnatural in the mini-landscapes I try to create in my troughs. A small square of plastic window screen over the trough drainage holes prevents soil from washing out and bugs from getting in. One 3-foot-square screen section (available in hardware or home supply stores) has lasted me for years.

I fill the container no more than three-quarters full of soil, and then add my accent rocks, trying to duplicate a natural formation. The number of stones and the style depends on individual preference; I like an odd or asymmetrical style. In any case, it looks more natural if the stones match or are close to the color of the trough.

Once the stones are in, I place the plants in the remaining spaces, without putting any plant smack in the middle of a space to avoid the "sore thumb" look. I water the trough slowly and gently, and then top-

In the center of the ruin floor sits one of the first hypertufa troughs I made. Because of its size, I raised it up on blocks so it would not look so heavy, and I also like the tiered effect this offers.

The same pot, same location, in different seasons: In March **(upper left)**, we used *Helleborus* ×*nigercors* 'Pink Frost' underplanted with moss and decorated with pinecones. In May **(upper right)**, the pot was replanted with *Allium karataviense* and *Sedum rupestre* 'Angelina'. And in June **(bottom left)**, we moved on to spurges, with *Euphorbia milii* and *E. hypericifolia* 'Inneuphe' (sold under the name 'Diamond Frost'). Yellow *Corydalis lutea* is growing in the gravel around the pot.

Opposite, top: Color pots can hold multiple or single plants. And in either case, the pots can be grouped and regrouped to provide interesting combinations.

Opposite, bottom: Pots sometimes do not have to be pots; they can be anything that contains soil. Drain holes are provided in this wood block planted with colorful specimens of *Echeveria*.

COLOR POTS

Besides our collection of troughs, which are permanently planted, we have a large collection of container plants—different forms of *Agave*, *Primula*, *Eucomis*, *Camellia*, *Sansevieria*, and *Clivia*, as well as ferns, orchids, and many more—that we use as accents or in groupings throughout the garden. We also create what we call "color pots"—large containers overflowing with colorful plants that are changed as many as five or six times a year, depending on the whim of the moment. The pots are mainly Michael's baby, though sometimes I will create a container or two if I want to try what I think will be a particularly good combination. We plant these pots behind the scenes, in the nursery area, and use a ball cart—an oversized dolly designed for moving trees with their large root balls but perfect for moving heavy containers—to move them to their appointed places on our garden stage. Sometimes the pots have anchor plants and only one or two plants are switched out with each season; other times the entire pot is changed.

These pots allow us to bring favorite plants, such as snowdrops and hellebores, closer to eye level, which visitors to the garden especially enjoy. We can also play with color combinations that we might not be ready to commit to the ground. Many of the plants used in the color pots are subsequently moved into the nursery bed to await a permanent place in the garden, and the potting mix is refreshed and reused from year to year. We try to waste nothing.

BORDER LAYERS

To describe the sequence of bloom in just one of the densely planted borders in the heart of the garden would be complicated and perhaps confusing to the reader. A better read on the individual borders is provided in the photographs and captions, especially in those sequences that show the same border over a year. Taking a broader view, I can describe how the beds follow one another, and talk about some of the major features.

My goal has been to make sure the borders do not all peak at once, but instead to spread out the excitement from spring through fall. The first border to come into peak bloom, in March, is the formal hellebore garden, which is the closest to the house. The next borders to peak, which are very visible and thus very important, are the north border and then the west

vegetable garden border; because we can always see these two beds, they are kept at a high level of interest until frost cuts them down. The rose beds, first with peonies and then with roses, are the next to peak, followed by the south border of the vegetable garden in the summer, and finally the south border in the fall.

Layering speaks to diversity; every border has its layers, and each layer has many plants, some of which are stars and others simply supporting players. From a distance, only the taller stars in these beds are discernible—the roses, or foxgloves, or alliums, or lilies, depending on the season. Only on a stroll down the paths between the borders do the smaller plants, the subtleties and details, the combinations of colors and shapes and textures that make up each layer, become apparent.

dress it with stone dust or aquarium gravel—again trying to match the color of the trough and accent stones. Like the pebbles do in my ruin garden, this inorganic top-dressing keeps organic matter away from the crowns of the plants, decreasing the risk of fungal problems.

Most alpine plants naturally grow in lean soil, so only occasional feedings are necessary. When and if plants outgrow the trough, they can be divided. If they die, which plants do (especially alpine plants, which can be particularly fussy when grown outside their native haunts), the plants can be removed, and another specimen tried—perhaps in a different soil mix or in a different exposure. In troughs, as in the garden beds, I give any plant up to five chances to live before I give up and start looking for a replacement that will work with me instead of against me.

THE HEART OF THE GARDEN

At the heart of the garden, we have created a series of interconnected ornamental borders arrayed around the vegetable garden, which sits in the sunniest part of the property. With the exception of the south border, here the shape of the beds, unlike the other parts of the garden, is formal and geometric, which helps contain the exuberant plantings. These beds showcase some of my favorite flowers—peonies, roses, irises, lilies, hellebores, foxgloves, thistles, tulips, phlox, selections of *Patrinia*, *Vernonia*, and *Rudbeckia* . . . and so many others. It is difficult for me to play favorites, and not just because I am an equal-opportunity plantaholic who falls head over heels for almost any plant that loves this garden. Every plant in these beds was chosen to play a starring role in its particular place at a particular time—for example, the species peonies to provide early spring color, and the vernonias to provide height, color, and interest in later summer and fall—and to do without any of them would lessen the garden's overall beauty.

The Vegetable Garden and Its Borders

When the garden was two years old, I visited one of the original family homesteads outside Lederach, Pennsylvania, to see what influences I might learn from it. About 300 years ago, Dielman Kolb (Culp is the anglicized version of this surname) came from Germany to join the growing community in and around Germantown, now a section of Philadelphia. His homestead, now in private hands but listed on the National Register of Historic Places, included a stone farmhouse, and the owners at that time still maintained the traditional four-square vegetable garden surrounded by a picket fence. As soon as I saw it, I knew that I had to have just such a garden at the heart of my place. I had already begun the

Opposite: Troughs can work in a variety of light conditions, with shade being the road less traveled. This trough for part shade includes dwarf hostas, *Iris cristata*, and a golden leaf bellflower, *Campanula portenschlagiana* 'Aurea'.

I feel that double borders should talk to each other. Here the foxgloves, alliums, and forget-me-nots are repeated in both the north border and the nearby border of the vegetable garden. The rose beds are barely visible in the background, enticing visitors to further explore.

north border then, and I saw how this vegetable bed could anchor a complete set of double borders covering all four points of the compass.

Beyond the practical design inspiration it gave me, the Kolb Homestead exuded an aura of comfortable hominess (which the Pennsylvania Germans call *Gemütlekeit*) that I knew would be a perfect fit for both my personality and my evolving garden style. This garden could be beautiful and utilitarian. It could continue a tradition that stretched back through my parents and grandparents, who all had vegetable gardens, to the beginnings of our family in this country. I could think of no better way to emphasize my belief that gardens are all about nurturing—not only how we nurture the plants we grow, but how they nurture us, both our bodies and our souls. I began putting in the vegetable garden, complete with the white picket fence, the following year.

The vegetable garden within the fence and the four ornamental borders that surround it are an exercise in formal geometry. To get the scale of the garden right, I matched its size and alignment to the footprint of the house. Each of the four squares within the fence are further divided into four more squares, making sixteen little beds in all. Paths between the beds are mulched with salt hay (a salt-tolerant hay that grows in seashore areas); it does not harbor troublesome weed seeds found in other hays, like wheat hay. The beds are fed with aged cow manure and leaf mold, the crops are rotated to avoid diseases, and hardly any pesticides are used. This garden does not feed us throughout the year, as it must have done for my ancestors, but our harvests enhance both our diet and our lives. Well into the fall we are still harvesting Brussels sprouts and kale from this garden, both of which look better and taste sweeter after being hit with a light frost. Then, after the first hard frost takes these plants down, the beds are cleaned up for winter, to rest until the following spring.

Just because a vegetable garden is utilitarian does not stop us from playing with design and color here as well. Four bamboo tepees, the fence pickets, and an arbor over the entrance add vertical interest as well as places to grow climbing plants. Color pots are set at the terminal points of the four main paths. In general, since the beds inside the fence cannot be viewed from the outside, the colors we use can be brighter than those used elsewhere, which always surprises visitors when they step inside. Yellow pole beans and yellow tomatoes, bull's blood beets, purple and white eggplant, red and green lettuces, the grays and purples of cabbage, kohlrabi, and kale—all these and more can be combined and contrasted just as in ornamental borders. The best thing about designing a vegetable garden is that if any combination fails to please, you can eat your mistakes.

The ornamental borders outside the picket fence are designed to complement the larger borders across from them. On the north and west sides, the plants and colors are complementary to the main north border. The fence and the entry arbor support clematis and old roses, including the antique Bourbon *Rosa* 'Climbing Souvenir de la Malmaison' and a

The stone birdbath from England echoes the four-square design of the vegetable beds. The chives, an edible form of *Allium*, are every bit as beautiful as their ornamental cousins.

Formality is alive and well in the vegetable garden, with its straight lines and square beds. It is our job as gardeners to make the formal beautiful and playful as well.

This page, top: (left) The borders around the vegetable garden reflect the change of seasons: irises, foxgloves and forget-me-nots in spring (right), and *Patrinia*, Joe-Pye weed, and *Phlox paniculata* in high summer.

Bottom: As the year progresses into fall, the colors and textures become bolder, with the additions of tender plants including cannas, elephant ears, and angel's trumpet (*Brugmansia* species).

Next page, clockwise: Vegetables also feed our appetite for beauty, with the beautiful colors and shapes of kohlrabi and cardoon, the flowers of pea vines, and the crinkly texture of Savoy cabbage leaves.

This page: The south border of the vegetable garden is different in height and bloom time from the other borders, with more purple and yellow used. As visitors walk around the garden, I want them to have a variety of experiences as they turn each corner; varying plant height and color are good ways to achieve this.

Opposite: By summer, the borders around the vegetable garden grow tall and hide it from view, until one passes through the arbor that marks the entryway.

Lilies are the star of the garden in the summer months, replacing foxgloves and irises; their one-upmanship is their delightful fragrance. *Lilium* 'Casa Blanca' echoes the white house (which is the English translation of its cultivar name), as well as the white picket fence and shed (visible in the background).

newer shrub rose, 'Sarah Van Fleet'. Grasses anchor two corners, providing a little looseness and naturalism in this area of geometric beds. The west side of the garden is shadier than the others, and I use architectural plants here, and foliage contrasts to compensate for lessened floral effect. The south side is brighter, with more yellows and other bright colors. Located at the bottom of a gentle slope, it is also a little wetter and thus hospitable to plants that may require more moisture to thrive.

The east side (or the back, when viewed from the house) is home to *Paeonia lactiflora* varieties and German iris, which are a features of late spring, as well as a variety of tall perennials that come on in the summer. The colors in this area reflect those of the north border and the adjacent rose garden.

When the foxgloves are finished blooming in June, we pull them out and place bananas in the empty spaces. Their large leaves offer a bold shape and combine well with the flowers of a *Sanguisorba* selection and several forms of *Rudbeckia*. Tropical plants work well in the hot summers of the mid-Atlantic region, when the temperature often tops ninety degrees with jungle-like humidity.

The North Border

When I think of one "rule" of gardening—that a border should be narrow enough so you do not have to step in to maintain it—I look at my north border and laugh. The first of my ornamental borders to be established, and still the largest, it is a rectangle 40 feet long and 14 feet wide. The border is backed by a clipped holly hedge, behind which is the hillside, making the bed seem like a mini hillside itself. This illusion is amplified by the tall plants in the border, and the fact that the bed was on a slight slope to begin with and mounded up even more before planting, putting many of the plants at eye level. The mounding contributes to the enclosed feeling of this part of the garden, and by using tall specimens (I am six-feet-two, but still the plants tower over me), I feel enveloped and almost overwhelmed by it. It is as if I am a child again, walking through the borders and staring up at the flowers in awe. Instead of creating a "choir" effect—with tall in the back, medium in the middle, and short in the front—I find that a flexible height line can be more dramatic. Having some taller "see-through" plants in front, such as bronze fennel or *Thalictrum rochebrunianum* 'Lavender Mist', can act as a veil, offering tantalizing hints of the plants hiding behind or below.

Because of its location as well as its size, this border is one of the most visible on the property. We see it (along with the west side of the vegetable garden) every time we come in the house, so both of these beds are intensively planted and carefully maintained. The north border, as with all the beds around it, gets a straight edging with an edging spade at least once a year, where the border meets the lawn, creating an unwavering line that helps unify the garden.

When I first started this bed, I kept it tame and pastel, with few bright colors. It was the fashion then, and I was still learning that it is okay to buck trends. I remember looking at the bed during its first full year of bloom, and thinking that if a garden reflects its creator, this border made

Before I put in the north border, the space was simply more lawn on which the bulldogs could play.

me look like I was unexciting, too safe in my choices. I soon began putting in brighter colors and bolder plants, which have made me happy ever since.

Among the plants in this border are old roses and Siberian iris, planted in more or less a straight line. Loose drifts of other plants appear natural but, as in other areas of the garden, are carefully placed and edited. The bed is mostly perennials, which makes it very old-fashioned and very high maintenance. The changing nature of perennials allows for changes of mood and expression as the plants emerge, come into flower, and then fade. A small portion of the bed is left to be filled with colorful annual and tender plants that are changed with the season, including digitalis, sweet alyssum, and forget-me-nots in the spring, followed by petunias (like *Petunia integrifolia*), *Phormium* selections, and cannas in the summer.

The dark green of the evergreen holly hedge—the second attempt at a hedge in this location—offers a strong backdrop to the bed's brighter colors as well as a contrasting texture. To keep the hedge lush and full, I make sure to keep the growth at the back of the border a couple of feet away, so sunlight can reach down to the bottom branches, keeping those branches full of leaves. For the same reason, I also selectively trim the hostas growing on the north side of the hedge.

The original hollies were small plants, a nursery's fall closeouts purchased at a very reduced price. They had no name tags but I knew they would provide the needed effect once they grew up. Later, when people would admire the hedge and ask me the cultivar, all I could tell them was that it was *Ilex* 'Two Dollars and Fifty Cents'.

For many years the hedge did well, but after a particularly dry summer a few years ago, some of the plants started dying. Then the $2.50 joke was on me. In search of replacements, I went around to nurseries with branches from my plants, trying without success to find a match. I finally went to the nursery where I suspected the plant was introduced, and there I got the bad news: the cultivar was obsolete and production had been discontinued years ago.

The only solution was to replace the entire 50-feet-long row of 4-feet-high hollies—not with small plants this time, but with plants of equal size, because twenty years had passed, I had matured along with the garden and was no longer willing to wait years for them to grow up. To justify the expense, I have convinced myself that the new plants are nicer, a deeper green, and at least now, when somebody asks, I can give them a real name: *Ilex* 'Blue Princess'.

While the hellebores are in their glory on the hillside in late February, March, and early April **(top)**, the north border and the other perennial beds closest to the house are resting. By May **(bottom)**, the north border has gained energy and color, which is carried through the fall.

Previous page: By the beginning of April (top), sweet alyssum gives a hint of what is to come in the borders, in particular the 'White Triumphator' tulips that will be blooming in the north border and in all the borders surrounding the vegetable garden a few weeks later. After the tulips, whose foliage is dying down naturally in the back of the bed, comes the moment for alliums (bottom), which bring an entirely different color and shape to the garden.

This page, top: At the beginning of June, more yellow appears in the north border: the spiky flowers are the native *Thermopsis caroliniana*; the purple spikes in the foreground are *Salvia nemorosa* 'Caradonna'.

Bottom: By August, the colors in the north border (on the east end) become much brighter and the planting style more ebullient. The phormiums are placed in a row in the bed, providing a constant color foil for drifts of other plants woven around them.

This page: *Digitalis purpurea,* the common foxglove, is a dramatic plant that I love. While they are biennial and do self-sow, I like to have more control over their placement, so I buy new plants every year when they are in bud and plant them after the tulips finish, placing them to look like they have self-sown.

Opposite: The north border in the fall is as much about textures of tropical plants, including the large, dangerous-looking spiny-leaved *Solanum quitoense,* as it is about saturated color combinations.

The Formal Hellebore Garden

I have had a long-time love affair with hellebores, some of which came with me when I moved back to Pennsylvania from North Carolina in 1988. But after starting the Brandywine Cottage garden, at first I only put them here and there around the house in a naturalistic fashion. Hellebores and other shade plants lend themselves to an informal planting style, and masses and drifts of them thrive on the hillside and elsewhere on the property.

Then I learned that one of England's great hellebore breeders, Helen Ballard, had created a dedicated hellebore border on her property. I had never considered this before, and at that point had never even seen such a border, but it immediately made perfect sense. As a designer, I could see that having so many in one space would make much more of a splash than having them dotted around. From a plant-lover's point of view, concentrating the plants in one bed would make it easier to appreciate these beauties when they bloomed.

My hellebore bed is a straight-edged rectangle and more tightly designed than my informal plantings. I placed it on the west side of the vegetable garden, close to the house so I could see it from inside. This placement also took advantage of the shade of existing trees, including several black walnuts, which can inhibit the growth of many plants but do not seem to bother hellebores.

My goal in this bed was to create a tapestry of colors when the plants are in bloom late February, March, and early April, an effect that is best viewed from higher points around the bed, especially from the second-story windows of the house. After the hellebore flowers fade at the end of April or early May, the other borders around the vegetable garden start coming into their own, with tulips and herbaceous perennials appearing. In the hellebore bed, foliage becomes just another feature in a textural collection of ferns, *Disporum* species, and other shade plants—a subtle but still beautiful blend of greens. (For more on hellebores, see chapter 3, page 199.)

Top: The hellebore bed, close to the house, is visible from the kitchen and dining room windows, and the view helps cheer me on during the winter months. All the plants in this bed were selected, sometimes by trial and error, to survive under black walnut trees.

Bottom: In the summer, the water feature provides habitat for frogs, which happen to be color-coordinated with the mostly green foliage in the hellebore bed at this season.

The water feature provides a contrast of shape in the rectangular border, and provides a mirror-like effect. In this view, the hillside is in the background.

After the hellebores bloom, green and creamy-white variegated foliage dominates this bed during the rest of the year, with hints of seasonal color in late spring, summer, and fall.

The Rose Beds

My two rose beds occupy a cozy spot at the east side of the garden. The first rose beds I created at Brandywine Cottage were a formal design, with roses only, each plant standing alone. Such beds, featuring single genera (peonies and irises are examples of other plants often given beds of their own), did not appeal to me when I saw them in the gardens of others, but books on roses seemed to feature this method of culture. This rose arrangement, however, satisfied neither the designer in me nor the collector. Compared to the commingling of plants in the rest of the garden, the roses cordoned off in their separate beds looked barren and forlorn.

After a few years, I realized that from a collector's standpoint, the bare ground beneath the bushes in the traditional rose garden was wasted space. So I began underplanting the roses with a variety of herbaceous perennials, extending the layers of interest of these beds. I also recognized that an additional advantage to mixed plantings with roses is the cover the perennials provide. Since I do not spray my roses because of the harmful effects of pesticides on the wildlife I love, my rose foliage is sometimes blemished by a fungus called black spot, which the perennials help to hide.

The first plants to bloom in the two rose beds, before the roses, in late April to early May, are the species and intersectional peonies. The acid-green flowers of *Euphorbia palustris* appear in April and last to late May or early June, and their color is echoed at ground level by the blooms of *Alchemilla mollis* and contrasted by the bronze foliage of *Geranium maculatum* 'Espresso'. Because lavenders (*Lavandula* species) do not like my garden's heavy soil, I use several forms of *Nepeta* to provide the same ethereal blue-green look, including *N.* ×*faassenii*, *N.* 'Joanna Reed', and *N. sibirica* 'Souvenir d'André Chaudron'. After the roses peak in June, the bed is overtaken by summer perennials, including *Patrinia scabiosifolia,* brightly colored forms of *Kniphofia* (including 'Ice Queen') and *Euphorbia corollata*, with its multitude of small, white, airy flowers (which I grow as a substitute for *Gypsophila paniculata*). In the spring, I edge the beds with old-fashioned, low-growing, white-flowered *Lobularia maritima;* after the sweet alyssum begins to fade in midsummer, I replace it with purple-flowered *Ruellia brittoniana*.

Opposite, and next two pages: The rose beds characteristically speak of color, but they have a certain unfolding, just like the roses themselves, getting more colorful and full as the season progresses. *Hakonechloa macra* 'All Gold', just emerging in the foreground of the first view in April and barely visible in the later view in June (page 141), is one of the few varieties of hakone grass that tolerates full sun, and provides me with a great color note to work with when the roses are out of bloom.

The two rose beds are in the back of the garden, barely visible from other areas and waiting to be discovered.

Opposite, top: This huge agave specimen anchors this rose bed and gives an immediate focal point; we place it there in early May, after the threat of frost has passed.

Bottom: Behind the rose beds and beyond the fence is the nursery area, with a cutting garden, hellebore seedling beds, a garden shed and compost pile, and a holding area for plants awaiting permanent homes in the garden.

This page: Rose season is past, but my desire for color remains. The towering yellow *Patrinia scabiosifolia* is talking to the hakone grass closer to the ground, with the white-blossomed hydrangea serving as a terminus for the path and toning down the yellows. This view looks north, between the two rose beds and up toward the hillside.

DESIGN LESSON
VERTICAL LAYERS

Layers in a garden can be at any level, not just on the ground. Colors that are high up, even in the trees, can be repeated below, at the middle or ground level, to give unity and balance to the garden, a border, or an arrangement. Roses are a perfect vehicle for this idea, sometimes carrying color up to the sky when grown on a fence, a wall, or any vertical structure.

In my rose pillar bed, roses climb on 8-foot-tall white wooden posts that are topped by finials. As with many vertical features, the rose pillars serve as exclamation points in the bed, drawing the eye of the viewer and announcing that something is back there worth exploring. Once the roses were fully established, the pillars also provided an opportunity to create interesting combinations at eye-level or higher. Clematis and honeysuckle vines clamber among the rose canes, providing additional lushness. To complete the picture, the pillars are underplanted with perennials.

What I have learned from my rose beds is that no space can get away with doing single duty in this garden. I am happiest when every space is layered with a succession of plants.

Left: The vertical shape of the grasses is repeated in the picket fence, the bamboo tepees, the rose pillars, the *Brugmansia* selection, and on up into the trees.

Right: The colors in the bold horizontal layer at the front of this bed (featuring purple-burgundy foliage of *Solanum quitoense* and vibrant chrysanthemums) are carried up into the foliage of the trees on the hillside.

The South Border

The undulating south border is the odd one out: it is kidney-shaped instead of square or rectangular like its neighbors. The front of the border is in the sun, and the back side is in the shade, giving it a split personality with which I am perfectly comfortable, being a Gemini myself. The least visible of the borders around the vegetable garden, it is simpler than the others and less intensively planted. It is also the last of these borders to peak, with fall bloomers including specimens of *Vernonia* and *Anemone*, *Solidago* 'Fireworks', and several *Sedum* varieties, including the reliable workhorse 'Autumn Joy'. Additional fall color is provided by the foliage of witch hazel and smoke tree (*Cotinus*), and perennials like *Amsonia hubrichtii* and *Ligularia dentata* 'Desdemona'. Because this border sits at the lowest part of the garden and also receives runoff from a neighbor's driveway, it is the only place in my mostly dry garden where I can grow Japanese and Louisiana irises.

It is my job as designer to make sure that all the pairs of borders that you walk through—so-called double borders—"talk to each other" in complementary rather than jarring tones, and that includes getting the south border in on the conversation. In spring, white *Cercis canadensis* var. *alba*, underplanted with white *Leucojum* selections, link to other beds with their masses of 'White Triumphator' tulips. The shady back of the border has a selection of trilliums and other spring ephemerals, epimediums, hakone grass, hostas, and hydrangeas. These plants reflect the adjacent shade garden, which hugs the entire southern boundary of the property, from the nursery area to the entry garden. In some ways, the more informal woodland feel of this shady part of the south border also reflects the hillside, on the opposite side of the garden but still in clear view, which serves to connect the heights of the garden with the low-lying part of the property.

In this bright October combination, the rose-pink *Anemone* ×*hybrida* 'Robustissima' underplanted with the purple *Lobelia* ×*speciosa* 'Vedrariensis' contrast with the gold-leaved hostas behind them and the *Hakonechloa macra* 'Albovariegata' in the foreground.

Opposite: *Solidago* 'Fireworks' signals the coming of autumn. The green elephant ear leaves provide a bold backdrop for the harmonizing gesture of the goldenrod.

This page, left: *Lobelia* ×*speciosa* 'Vedrariensis' does well in this fall border because it gets the moisture it loves. Here, it gives an analogous nod to the pale blue form of *Aster divaricatus*, an adaptable native plant that does well in many places in my garden.

Right: *Gentiana* 'True Blue' and *Sedum* 'Autumn Joy' make a stunning combination at the front of the south border.

The south border was created primarily to have a bed with a different season of interest from the north border. Here it is shown in a quiet moment in spring; fall is its strongest season.

Animals

My parents and grandparents fostered my love of the natural world in many ways, both by encouraging my love of plants and being indulgent when it came to my love of animals. Besides having many pets and my own livestock at my grandparent's farm, I used to bring home so many wild critters—from flying squirrels to turtles to horned toads and every living thing in between—that my mother later told me she was often afraid to look in my pockets.

All my life I have had English bulldogs as pets, short squat canines that are definitely an acquired taste. Michael and I now have two, Ella and her daughter, Dolly, who trundle around the property on their sturdy, short legs, sometimes content to sit in the sun, other times getting curious about insects and following them right into the garden beds unless we manage to collar the dogs first. A small tabby cat we named Hunter adopted us years ago, and she now lives the easy country life, sunning herself in warm weather and sleeping in her own heated bed in the barn during the winter months.

Chickens are the main livestock here, and to me they feel like a perfect fit for the cottage and its country garden. I raised them when I was a boy, and now have two different kinds of Bantams, Old English and Black Rosecomb. Both are on the small side, and they do not do much damage in the garden. The chickens provide us with eggs (about the size of small commercial eggs) and occasional baby chicks, and when we let them out into the garden they become moveable art, darting around, eating insects (a plus), and bringing a clucking vitality to the scene.

The chicken chalet, which is what we call their peak-roofed condominium, sits on the edge of the south border. Designed by the garden artist named Simple, it has legs to help protect the flock from earthbound predators such as foxes and raccoons. Avian predators also have to be watched for, especially red-tailed hawks. My birds are especially vulnerable in late winter, when the hawks have little else to eat and these small chickens are easy to spot and pick off because the trees have dropped their leaves. I usually keep them under lockdown at this time.

Opposite: The south border still has to relate to the rest of the garden even when it is not at its peak. Here, the blooms of the white-flowered form of Chinese redbud in mid-April reflect the white tulips and dogwoods blooming elsewhere. Beyond, *Cercis canadensis* 'Tennessee Pink' shows its bright, cheery colors.

This page: Ella, the garden overseer, is about the only resident of Brandywine Cottage who sits on the chaise lounge. The gardeners have little spare time for such relaxation.

Our garden is a Bantam chicken garden, not a peacock garden. My Black Rosecomb Bantams
are small enough not to crush the hellebores as they search for insects to eat.

THE HILLSIDE

As we have recreated it, the hillside, with its mixed border at the north edge, reminds me of the wild spaces that are a great part of who I am and what I love. Besides connecting me to the wild, it also protects the garden against encroachment from the modern world, represented by the subdivision that borders the property on two sides but which the hillside helps to hide. Even before I planted any of the gardens here, climbing up the hill immediately gave me different perspectives on the property below, providing new ideas and angles that I used in designing my beds and borders.

At the foot of the hillside, to retain the slope, we built a 360-foot rubble dry wall. We have moved every stone in this wall at least twice, and feel a kinship with the slaves who built the pyramids—or at least with a pair of pack mules. Today I might think twice about undertaking such a monumental task, but back then Michael and I were possessed by this project, often working into the night under the bright beams of the car headlights. Ah, the energy of youth—where has it gone? Into the accumulation of wisdom, I suppose, but that sometimes seems like paltry compensation when there are tough jobs in the garden that still need to be done.

The hillside faces south, which means that plants here come on much earlier than those in the lower part of the garden. This issue is both a blessing and a curse—good for the many winter-blooming plants that grow here but not so good when late frost hits—since often the more advanced plants on the hillside suffer most. Since the hillside is so visible when you enter the garden, it made sense to have it be the first area to come into bloom. It peaks while the gardens below are still dormant, its main show subsiding as the rest of the garden comes to life. This constant unfolding, where we continually have something new to look forward to, is what I love about a garden, and about life.

Clearing the Hillside

Although it took up half of the 2-acre property, the hillside was not high on the list when I started the garden. I had plenty to do closer to the house and in the more accessible areas on the flat acre around it. The hillside seemed so daunting that well-meaning friends advised me to leave it be, telling me that it was too steep, too dry, too overgrown with invasive plants to maintain any kind of garden there. This advice only steeled my resolve to eventually do something with the hillside, and not only to prove to them that I could. I did not purchase the property to leave half of it fallow.

Having Michael come to live at Brandywine Cottage was a godsend for the garden in many ways, but especially for our work on the hillside. I am not saying I would have never tackled it without him, but Michael did

Opposite: These three views show the progression of growth in one section of the hillside, from late March to late May. Because I see this view every time I go in and out of the house, I want it to be more dynamic than other less visible garden areas. The bright yellows and whites of the daffodils (top) gradually yield to the pastels of spring (bottom, left). In the final view (bottom, right), *Styrax japonica* in full bloom is underplanted with drought-tolerant blue-leaved cultivars of *Hosta sieboldiana*.

most of the work clearing this large space, which allowed creating a garden there much sooner than I would have on my own. Underneath a canopy of native trees—locust, American elm, tulip poplar, cherry, redbud, and dogwood—was a tangled understory of invasive plants and shrubs that had to be completely removed before any kind of garden could be created here. Particularly troublesome were two invasives, *Rosa multiflora* and *Lonicera japonica*, which had draped themselves over everything. Poison ivy, a native plant whose berries are a favorite food of some birds, also grew everywhere, and to me it seemed the most virulent strain in the world—I had never gotten a rash from this plant until I moved here.

The easiest way to rid ourselves of this mess would have been to spray it all with herbicide, making several applications over time to be sure that everything was truly dead. Because of the harm we believe that such chemicals can do, we decided against this option, and chose instead to do the work by hand. Michael ended up clearing the entire hillside several times, both with a weed whacker and by hand, pulling and digging, before we planted anything. The weeds are still a constant battle, one that we cannot let go for too long, but we believe that the ecological benefits of doing the job ourselves, rather than letting the chemicals do it for us, were worth every minute of the extra work.

This bench is one of several on the approximately one-acre hillside.

At the end of June, after a brief rest the hillside comes alive again with the blooming of the hydrangea collection. I have been surprised by how many hydrangeas will tolerate the dryness of the hillside.

Replacing the Understory and Herbaceous Layers

We left most of the trees on the hillside, but when we were done with the work of clearing, the shrub layer and the herbaceous ground layer were gone. Some people might be satisfied with a woodland that emulates a Gothic cathedral—a towering canopy of trees, underplanted with moss—but we were trying to recreate the natural world, so we knew we would have to replant all the layers we took out.

We had cleared the hill in vertical sections, and we replanted each section in the same way, each vertical slice of the hill having its own color theme, with each theme transitioning softly into the other and also relating to the garden as a whole. As we planted we did not amend the soil, only top-dressed with the leaves that are any woodland's natural fertilizer. Adding too much nitrogen causes plants to stretch, sometimes beyond their means, and on a south-facing hillside where the plants would already be reaching for the light, this would make them more likely to flop. The soil is clayey and dry, and since we rely on a well for our water supply, we do not give the plants extra water once they are established. Just as we do in the ruin garden, we like to get new plants on the hillside into the ground early, so they have the cool weather and rainfall of spring to establish themselves before the onset of the summer heat.

The hillside's deciduous tree canopy is ideal for spring-flowering bulbs such as snowdrops and narcissus, and spring ephemerals such as trilliums and fawn lilies (*Erythronium* species). Hellebores do well, as do

This page: *Hepatica* is another genus of woodland jewels; I do not know how many I have in my collection, but I know it is not enough. *Hepatica transsilvanica* **(left)** has electric blue flowers, each slightly bigger than a quarter. And the *H. japonica* hybrid, from Japan **(right)**, reminds me of a miniature camellia.

Opposite: From the many paths on the hillside—none of which is visible from the garden below—we get an elevated perspective of the beds, and feel as if we are both floating above and enveloped by our creation.

hostas and many other herbaceous plants I love. Many of these ground-layer plants were placed in naturalistic drifts to make it appear as if they were sowing themselves. The existing native plants, including flowering dogwood (*Cornus florida*) and eastern redbud (*Cercis canadensis*), suggested that other species and cultivars of these genera might do well here. I now have collections of both, and magical are the early spring days when the pink and white blooms of these two small trees overlap. I have always loved magnolias, and what was supposed to be a sunny part of the hillside has now become shady as I add to my collection of these small trees. It turned out that hydrangeas thrive on the hillside, and my collection of *Hydrangea* species and cultivars is a summertime delight. Witch hazels are a winter highlight, and many specimens also have colorful fall foliage. Other herbaceous and woody plants help fill out the layers, and more are added every year.

Much of the preliminary work on the hillside is no longer apparent, which is proper in a finished garden. Just as most visitors to the garden rarely picture all the work leading up to the crescendo of a particular border—the initial turning over and enriching of the soil, the planting, the editing, the constant maintenance—neither do they imagine that this hillside is not just the work of Mother Nature, with a few tweaks and embellishments by us. I feel complimented by such misperceptions. My goal, after all, was to make the hillside appear natural. But I am also glad I saved pictures of this process, if only to serve as a reminder of how far we have come, and how much of the resulting beauty is at least partly to our credit.

Having a wooded area means that we need shade plants to fill it up. Among my many favorite genera for the understory are *Polygonatum* and *Disporum*, not only for their flowers but for their architectural shapes. This plant is a yet-to-be-named yellow-foliage form of *Polygonatum*.

Top: I found this hardy
specimen of *Disporum* in
Japan. It was introduced by
Sunny Border Nurseries as
'Dancing Geisha'.

Bottom: This crested form
of *Polygonatum* has crisply
pleated leaves.

HILLSIDE LAYERS

The hillside is the earliest part of the garden to bloom, and holds the bulk of the winter interest, starting with witch hazels and snowdrops in February, followed by hellebores and daffodils in March and April. Early flowering rhododendron varieties overlap with the daffodils, and a special show is put on by nearly twenty specimens of the purple-flowered *Rhododendron* 'Olga Mezitt'. After a brief lull, in which the textures of hostas, disporums, and other foliage plants are the main feature, the hillside peaks again with the blooms of the hydrangea collection beginning in June.

The hillside layers can also be seen as vertical bands of color, starting at the western end with yellows, moving to a section of purples that play off the foliage of *Cercis canadensis* 'Forest Pansy', to a section that is mainly green, then to a band featuring gray and white foliage colors

on the eastern end. These color bands are not obvious, since I tried to blend them one into the other when they were planted, and they have blended themselves even more in subsequent years. Native azaleas and *Hydrangea quercifolia* have been planted to make broad gestures, with dozens of both used to unify this large space.

On the hillside I have strived to create a stylized woodland, trying to hide the hand of the designer and let nature speak. In early April **(left)**, *Magnolia ×soulangeana* is underplanted with daffodils and black hellebores. Three weeks later **(right)**, highlights are *Rhododendron* 'Olga Mezitt', black hellebores, and *Symphytum azureum*.

CHAPTER THREE

SIGNATURE PLANTS THROUGH *the* SEASONS

IN THE GARDEN, I EXPRESS MYSELF IN TWO DISTINCT ways: as a plantsman who enjoys collecting specimens of a variety of genera and watching how they grow and express themselves, and as a designer who enjoys playing with plants to achieve a desired effect. Negotiating between these two sides of my gardening self is sometimes as tricky as walking a tightrope, but I would not have it any other way. And unlike other collectors, who sometimes express a little embarrassment or shame when discussing this issue with nonbelievers, I am proud to announce to the world: Hello, my name is David, and I am addicted to plants.

A COLLECTOR'S PASSIONS

When it comes to plant collecting, my thoughts might be summed up in seven simple words: If one is good, more is better. Many of my plant collections began as one species that did well for me. My theory is that if I like you, I will like your genus and your family and invite many of them over as well. Of course, when everyone sits down at the table, I may have a little sorting out to do. Not everyone needs to be planted by the front door; some may end up out back; perhaps a few failures even farther back, buried in the compost pile. But there will always be those stars that do end up on center stage, and other rarities and oddities that I might tuck in secret places, only sharing these gems with people who I know will appreciate them.

The simple joy of growing something you love is one of the common denominators of gardening; I just tend to spread my love around to more plants than the average person. In many ways, my passion for collecting feeds the designer in me, by giving me more raw material to work with. It helps reduce my carbon footprint, by replacing in my garden what has been lost in much of the world around me. My plants help me make the world a more beautiful place, and give me exercise and fresh air and keep me in touch with nature.

I was exposed to plant collecting at an early age, with one grandmother collecting begonias, the other madly in love with her roses. No wonder that collecting felt like a natural thing for me to do, once I had a garden of my own. I first began collecting daffodils, because they bloomed earlier than any other plant I knew of at that time. I could never have foreseen how far that first impulse would take me, to the discovery of plants that bloom earlier, and earlier, until I had a collection that confounded any conception of early or late, since I have now have many plants in bloom every month of the year.

Beauty is the main driver of my collecting, my twin desires to have a beautiful collection of individual plants and to combine them in beautiful ways in the garden. The more individuals I have, the more rich and layered the overall composition becomes. I suppose what I am really addicted to is beauty, as manifested in the world of plants.

My father played football in high school, and I think he was always a bit disappointed that I never played this sport when I came of age. I sometimes half-jokingly call plant collecting a competitive sport, and perhaps it is my version of football, an activity through which I have made many friends and gained a sense of personal accomplishment. My memberships in societies devoted to specific types of plants (such as the American Daffodil Society) or specific techniques (such as the International Plant Propagators Society) or gardening in specific regions (such as the Hardy Plant Society/Mid-Atlantic Group) has been like going to graduate school, and has only increased my devotion to this "sport." What I love about horticulture is that there is no possibility of ever knowing it

Previous: When in doubt, use blue. The pale blue flowers of *Symphytum azureum*, for instance, bring the color of the sky right down to the earth.

Opposite: I first saw *Hacquetia epipactis* at the Elizabeth Miller Garden in Seattle, Washington, and fell in love its bright chartreuse flowers. Its late March bloom time is an added bonus.

all; there is always more to learn, and there are always more people to learn from.

When people visit my garden, I want them to feel that the garden is approachable on all different levels so even beginners can learn from it. I want visitors to have an emotional reaction, both to the garden as a whole and to the beauty of individual plants. On a deeper level, I also want them to have an intellectual appreciation for how we garden here. If someone wants to come to the garden and simply enjoy the view or the foxgloves, they surely can. If they want to go deeper and learn how I rotate out the foxgloves or why I chose to put this plant with that one, I can tell them about that. And if they are plant nerds like I am, we can discuss the traits I select for in my hellebore breeding, or whether the ovary on this *Galanthus* specimen is more rounded than that on its neighbor. My goal in sharing the garden is to teach others, gently. And as long as visitors go home and garden, I consider it a win.

In the sections that follow, I describe some of the garden's signature plants—why I love them and what they contribute to the garden at the peak of their season.

Opposite, top: *Anemonella thalictroides* f. *rosea* 'Oscar Schoaf' is prized by rock gardeners because of its long bloom time (April–May) and double pink flowers. Although it looks like it might be finicky, I have found it easy to grow.

Bottom: I received this *Cardamine quinquefolia* specimen from one of my hellebore mentors, Elizabeth Strangman, who collected it in China. It blooms with my hellebores, and although it may look a little thuggish, it is well-behaved, going dormant in the summer. This charming, little-known plant could be used more often in our gardens.

This page: In my opinion, *Adonis amurensis* 'Flore Pleno' needs a sexier name, since it is a star of the garden when it blooms in late winter.

WINTER

One group of plants that have always fascinated me are those that have an off-peak bloom time—late summer or autumn, or even winter—because they help me extend the gardening season beyond its generally accepted bounds. Though I spent about half my life in the South, I do not like summer heat, and much prefer being outdoors in the cooler and even cold months of the year. For this reason alone it made sense, once I moved back up north, that I did not want to stop gardening at the traditional time for this region, usually by the end of October and certainly before Thanksgiving. To then wait five months before starting up again in March or April seemed an unbearably long hiatus to me. I enjoy sitting by the fireplace reading nursery catalogs as much as anyone, but for *five months?* I have trouble sitting still for five minutes! My choice was no choice at all, really: either I could suffer all winter from cabin fever, or I could create a garden that would get me out of the house twelve months of the year, giving me worthwhile work to do and allowing me to continually exercise my passion for plants.

If I had to pick two signature genera for Brandywine Cottage, out of all the ones we grow, they would have to be *Galanthus* and *Helleborus*, more commonly known as snowdrops and hellebores. These are plants with moxie, and being a gardener of the same spirit, I cannot help but love them. They are Jack Frost's nemeses, daring the winter weather to nip them as they bloom against the odds in the coldest months of the year.

Hellebores and snowdrops are what I call "participatory plants"—you have to touch them to truly enjoy them. I like that their flowers seem simple but are actually full of subtlety and nuance. They draw you in, they seduce you, they do not tell you everything about themselves in the first five minutes; they only reveal their true personalities upon close examination, since the inside of the flower is often where the action is. I like being seduced, by plants and by gardens. I have tried to make my garden seductive, its multiple layers like multiple personalities, only revealing themselves under careful analysis and over time. The more you look, the more you see, the more you fall in love.

Snowdrops and hellebores are two great genera for the winter garden; but two genera do not a garden make, not even in the most difficult gardening season for those of us in temperate climates. Even in winter, when the weather could provide me with an easy excuse, I will not take no for an answer; I am not content to have only a garden of collections. I wanted my snowdrops and hellebores to be part of a coherent and layered design, which meant I had to find other plants to accompany them. This led me to the bright yellow flowers of *Adonis* and *Eranthis* selections, to early blooming forms of *Narcissus* and *Crocus*, and other late-winter perennials and bulbs. I found a host of winter-blooming shrubs, including witch hazel, wintersweet, and *Jasminum nudiflorum*—all with yellow flowers to brighten up the grayest of winter days. Others have colorful twigs like

The warm-toned bark of *Cornus sanguinea* 'Midwinter Fire' shines in the late winter morning sun.

Opposite: The dried flowers of *Hydrangea petiolaris* are a bit tattered but still beautiful in early March.

This page, top: Winter interest sometimes comes in shades of browns and grays. Even after a long winter, a rose hip is a still a rose hip.

Bottom: The exfoliating bark of *Acer griseum* lends texture to the garden.

the red and yellow twigged *Cornus* cultivars, and various species of *Rubus*, with their ghostly white brambles. Many evergreen shrubs or trees also play a role, providing a backdrop for other plants and, when the garden is buried in snow, offering a green reminder, in an otherwise whited-out world, that there is still life out in the garden.

I also learned to appreciate the nonflowering and, in some cases, non-living plant parts that ornament the garden in winter. The exfoliating bark of trees like stewartia and *Acer griseum*, beautiful in any season, is especially notable after the leaves fall and the garden goes quiet. Berries and seed pods give color and form to the garden, at least until the birds devour them; grasses can be attractive for a time, sometimes all winter if successive snows do not flatten them. Dried hydrangea flowers take on a special beauty this time of year; another person might see them as simply tattered and finished, but I love their delicate, lacy quality. All of these add interest to the scene, even if they are just a dormant plant's fading parts that have managed to hang on through the wind and cold. And then, as spring gets nearer, many signs appear—the swelling buds of shrubs and trees and the emerging stems and leaves of herbaceous plants breaking dormancy—announcing that the relative peace of the garden in winter is about to explode back into life.

I like the gardens closest to the house to bloom first, so we can appreciate them from inside and on quick outdoor visits in cold weather. But it also helps to have some winter interest away from the house, to force you outside to explore. The siren song of a plant in bloom has lured me across oceans and my frozen garden alike. On New Year's Day, I always give myself the special challenge of making an arrangement for the dinner table. If the snow is deep, this might be nearly impossible, but in a good year I can bring in the flowers of hellebores, winter jasmine, and various *Galanthus* species.

With winter gardening, it is particularly useful to be intimately knowledgeable with your site, in order to locate warmer areas (like my south-facing hillside) that will bring plants into bloom earlier, and sheltered areas that may help borderline-hardy plants survive. *Edgeworthia chrysantha*, with clusters of fragrant white flowers with yellow centers, is a late-winter blooming shrub supposedly hardy only to zone 7b. For years I grew it in a pot that we brought inside in cold weather, until it got so big that I had to find a place for this gem in the ground. I planted it in a warm spot against the southwest corner of the house, where it has survived now for more than seven years.

To me, the winter does not end on the March equinox; it continues until early or mid April, when the threat of frost is almost gone and spring has undeniably arrived. Then the work starts to pile up for us, both professionally and at the cottage, until by June and July the garden can feel like a runaway circus train about to fly off the tracks. At those times I often long for winter—not for the fireplace and its nearby stack of catalogs, but for the slower pace and simpler garden of that time of

The nuanced beauty of a dried bract of a translucent seed head of *Perilla frutescens*, as seen against a backdrop of snow, is more interesting to me than the flowers themselves.

year. Often winter is the only time I can be out in my garden and actually take a deep breath, relax, see where the garden is, and imagine how much farther I might be able to take it. Just as the gardening year never ends for me, neither do my dreams.

Galanthus

When late-winter cabin fever has me in its bitter grip, snowdrops remind me that earthly energy still flows. These diminutive bulbs, members of the amaryllis family, are understated and refined, yet their pristine white flowers contrasted against the bare, dull winter ground give them an eye-popping allure. Species such as *Galanthus reginae-olgae* start blooming in October, and other species and selections extend the snowdrop season through April. Remarkably hardy and resilient, they even bloom beneath a blanket of snow if they have to.

Galanthus nivalis, the common snowdrop, is the most shade-tolerant and also among the later blooming, and I have planted masses of it on the hillside. But I greatly prefer the form of the earlier blooming giant snowdrop, *Galanthus elwesii*, which has larger flowers and more interesting variants. Named after Henry John Elwes, a plantsman who collected them in Turkey, *G. elwesii* was introduced into commercial trade in England in the 1870s. Visitors can still see Elwes's wonderful garden, including his collection of *Galanthus* selections, at Colesbourne Park in central England, where his descendants still live.

I use forms and crosses of *Galanthus elwesii* and other virtuosos in my collection along the edge of pathways or as exclamation points at the front of borders, where their differences can be readily examined and appreciated. To the beginner, all snowdrops look rather similar. It took time for me to learn to recognize those tiny distinguishing features—the sinus markings, the angle of the flower, the height of the ovary above the foliage. One of my favorites is G. ×*hybridus* 'Robin Hood', which presents its single flowers at an unusual angle, with outer petals that are long and elegantly tapered with a little X in the middle of the inner petals. Some people see this marking as a pair of crossed sabers, but I see it as a kiss.

With a little practice, some varieties can be easily recognized while others remain tricky even for the experts. I have spent many cold days in the gardens of galanthophiles examining the flowers, trying to see what they see, and sharing my own interpretations. Fussing so over such small flowers might seem excessive to some, but it is my contention that this kind of close looking helps train our eyes to see subtle details and nuance everywhere in our gardens, a sharpening of vision that can only make us better gardeners.

My snowdrop collection includes more than a hundred different cultivars and is still growing. This makes it easier for me to attend the British *Galanthus* galas and luncheons in late winter; before I had gotten my collection up to fifty, nobody took me seriously. Many varieties are hard to

Opposite, clockwise:
Flashes of color are much appreciated in the cold months of the year: the bright red berries of *Rohdea japonica*; the surprisingly fragrant yellow and white flowers of *Edgeworthia chrysantha*, a daphne relative; the spritely golden blooms of *Adonis amurensis*; and the splash of pink offered by *Prunus mume* 'Peggy Clarke', a flowering apricot, in late March.

A selection of eleven snowdrop blossoms shows the subtleties of genus *Galanthus*: (clockwise from bottom right) *Galanthus nivalis* f. *pleniflorus* 'Lady Elphinstone', *Galanthus nivalis* f. *pleniflorus* 'Blewbury Tart', *Galanthus plicatus* 'Diggory', *Galanthus* 'Primrose Warburg', *Galanthus elwesii*

selection (unnamed), *Galanthus* 'Tubby Merlin', *Galanthus nivalis* 'Viridapice', *Galanthus elwesii* selection (unnamed), *Galanthus* ×*hybridus* 'Robin Hood', *Galanthus* 'South Hayes', *Galanthus plicatus* 'Augustus'.

Opposite, top: Winter weather hardly deters the aptly named snowdrop.

Bottom: A clump of *Galanthus nivalis* prospers with an equally intrepid winter-blooming companion, *Cyclamen coum*.

This page, top: Fortunately for me, *Galanthus* 'Primrose Warburg', with yellow ovaries and markings, increases well in my garden.

Bottom: I am not usually drawn to double snowdrops, but I love *Galanthus* 'Ballerina' for the regularity of its inner petals.

get, and maybe that is part of the thrill. Prices can be ridiculous because of their scarcity, but I consider them a worthwhile investment. Some I get by trading with other collectors—I received one rarity, 'Rosemary Burnham', in lieu of part of a lecture fee—but I have also paid from $20 to over $100 for a single snowdrop bulb. If you think that sounds crazy, let me put it this way: How many $20 meals have you completely forgotten? To me galanthus are unforgettable, and they also increase, unlike my 401(k) in recent years.

Galanthus largely come from the woodland edge and meadows in the Mediterranean region, specifically Iran, Turkey, and the Balkans. They like warm springs and dry summers, areas that are neither too wet nor too shady. The deciduous shade of our south-facing hillside is a good location for them, allowing them to send up their leaves, bloom, take in their nutrients, and go dormant before the overhanging trees and shrubs have leafed out. I have placed many *Galanthus elwesii* cultivars along the stone wall at the bottom of the hillside, a warm area where the snow melts first. They come into bloom early and, since this area is the first that anyone sees when they pull in the driveway, they put on a good early show.

I like the large, rounded, single flowers the best. I am very picky about doubles, preferring a consistent shape like a rose over a raggedy flower. I remain to be convinced about the beauty of most of the odd-looking cultivars, though I do grow a few for the sake of comparison with my ideal. I prefer plants with shorter leaves; to me the long, cabbagelike foliage on some varieties seems out of proportion and detracts from the flowers. Interesting sinus markings also catch my eye—the more different they are from the typical *Galanthus nivalis* marking, the better.

Companions for my snowdrops include *Cyclamen coum* and pale lavender *Crocus tommasinianus*. When I want some real drama, I match up *Galanthus elwesii* with a black-flowered *Helleborus orientalis*, a striking contrast that could have been dreamed up by Coco Chanel. I am currently adding rare cultivars with yellow markings and yellow ovaries, which I can play off other yellows found in the garden at this time of year, such as *Cornus sericea* 'Flaviramea', mahonia flowers, early daffodils, yellow-berried hollies, and yellow-flowered hellebores. Yellow is useful any time of the year: not only is it cheerful, but it also can provide a pleasing contrast.

A few years ago, walking with two of my galanthus mentors through a woodland in England carpeted with thousands of the typical green and white snowdrops, I managed to spot one with a yellow tip, glowing like a piece of gold on the forest floor. Yellow snowdrops are so rare and, at least among galanthophiles, so desirable, that I felt as if I had hit the lottery. We carefully collected it, and it was successfully propagated, and the question then was, "What do we call it?" I had wanted to call it 'Three Musketeers', to honor the three people involved in its discovery, but it was introduced at the 2009 Royal Horticultural Society Winter Show in England as *Galanthus* 'David L. Culp'. I have it in my garden, and I am proud that this elegant plant bears my name.

Galanthus 'South Hayes' is named after the garden of the late English galanthophile Primrose Warburg.

Opposite, clockwise:
Galanthus 'David L. Culp' is
a must-have plant, at least
for my garden. *Galanthus
elwesii* var. *monostictus* 'Deer
Slot' has markings that
resemble a deer's hoof print.

Galanthus plicatus 'Colossus'
is a strong-growing early
bloomer. This unnamed
seedling of *Galanthus
plicatus* 'Trym' has distinctive
green markings.

This page: *Galanthus
×hybridus* 'Robin Hood' has
markings like crossed sabers
or an X (for *kiss*).

This page: *Galanthus nivalis* is a good snowdrop for naturalizing; it reproduces quickly and is the least expensive.

Opposite: The flowers of *Galanthus plicatus* 'Diggory' resemble tiny Chinese lanterns.

SNOWDROP CULTURE

While galanthus have plenty of complementary companions, they perform best when free from overbearing neighbors that might out-compete them for nutrients or light in the growing season. One of the reasons I remove the old leaves of my hellebores in the winter is to provide light for the snowdrops I plant among them. Hostas are another good companion; as the snowdrop foliage is dying back, the hosta leaves emerge to hide this bit of garden unsightliness. Plants to avoid for snowdrop areas include those with dense carpets of roots, such as epimediums, through which the emerging leaves might have difficulty penetrating.

Congested clumps will need dividing to deter disease and the "encasing" of flowers, which prevents them from opening. While snowdrops can be moved "in the green," with the foliage still fresh, this can set the bulb back by damaging active roots. It is better to divide the clumps as the foliage goes dormant, indicating that they have finished their growth for the year. To feed my snowdrops, I use a fertilizer high in phosphorus and potassium and low in nitrogen. I only do this for very weak or very expensive ones, or those I want to increase more quickly. Some people who are more patient than I like to plant single bulbs and wait for the clumps to bulk up on their own. That is fine, if all you can get is one, but I like a minimum of three, better five, best ten: five bulbs planted in a tight drift, the rest drifting outward from the main drift as if they were spreading by themselves.

While most of the plants in my garden have no labels, I make an exception for my galanthus. Besides helping me keep their names straight, the labels also enable visitors to my garden learn which plants they like. I also keep a written record of where each one is planted, which is the best way to manage any collection of plants that go dormant and live underground for months of the year.

Galanthus elwesii 'Grumpy' has a frowning face.

Hellebores

In late winter and early spring, my hellebores take center stage. From this genus come some of the best perennials for shade—long lived, long blooming, evergreen, virtually disease free, and deer proof. They provide a wide range of colors at a time of the year in which gray and brown (and the white of an occasional snowfall) are the predominant tones in the landscape. Even when buried by snow, or laid low by a hard frost, these sturdy plants revive with the first warming rays of sun, like a flattened boxer rising from the mat. You simply have to love a plant that can take whatever punch the weather throws and still show off at that time of year.

Hellebores are members of the Ranunculaceae, or the buttercup family—not the rose family, as common names of the plant (Lenten rose, Christmas rose) misleadingly imply. This diverse family is one that loves my garden, and includes a number of other genera that I grow, among them *Adonis*, *Aquilegia*, *Clematis*, *Hepatica*, *Thalictrum*, and the family's namesake, *Ranunculus*.

The fifteen or so *Helleborus* species are divided into two main groups. The caulescent group (with leaves on their flowering stems) includes *H. argutifolius*, *H. foetidus*, *H. lividus*, and *H. vesicarius*. The larger acaulescent group (without leaves on their flower stems) contains all other species along with the Oriental hybrids (*Helleborus ×hybridus*). These hybrids are the most popular and easiest hellebores to grow, tolerating almost full sun to almost full shade (though the denser the shade, the fewer flowers they will produce). They generally prefer slightly neutral to acidic soils, and will tolerate dry shade far better than wet soil, in which they might rot.

I began growing hellebores when I lived down South, but did not start a serious collection until I moved back to Pennsylvania. In 1992, after visiting two of Germany's premier hellebore growers, Gisela Schmiemann and Günter Jürgl, I brought home several boxes loaded with their plants, and my relationship with hellebores moved from one of simple affection to true obsession. I soon began breeding my own hellebore strain (now sold under the trade name 'Brandywine Hybrids'). Since the mid-1990s, I have traveled to Europe almost every winter to select new plants to add to my breeding stock. In that time, Elizabeth Strangman, along with the staff at Ashwood Nursery, Blackthorn Nurseries, and Phedar Nurseries, and Thierry Delabroye (in addition to the aforementioned breeders), have generously shared their plants, knowledge, and encouragement. And along the way, as often happens in horticulture, our shared passion for this genus has also led to some lasting friendships.

I once thought I had to have a plant of every hellebore species, but finally came to the more sensible conclusion that I only needed to grow what I think are the best of them and their cultivars. I especially appreciate those with interesting foliage, like *Helleborus multifidus*, *H. argutifolius*, and *H. torquatus*, and plant them along the edges of pathways so their form and texture can be closely admired. *Helleborus niger* 'Potter's Wheel' is the earliest blooming variety in my garden, usually in flower around

Floating in a bowl of water, these blossoms display the color range and flower forms of my 'Brandywine Hybrid' hellebores.

Thanksgiving and sometimes in the company of early snowdrops, such as *Galanthus elwesii* var. *monostictus* 'Potter's Prelude' (no relation between either the plants or the people who introduced them). Crosses between *H. argutifolius* and *H. niger* have resulted in some interesting hybrids, grouped under the name *H. ×nigercors*. We use these plants in our color pots, where it is easier to appreciate the bright colors and the more formal shape of the flowers.

While hellebores often self-sow, I generally discourage this tendency by cutting off the seedpods. This not only keeps the garden tidy, but prevents seedlings from sprouting up in the crowns of other plants. And since I am a breeder, it also helps me limit the procreation happening in my beds; controlled crosses are the best way for me to maintain flower type and color. Hellebores do not need to be regularly divided, but as with many herbaceous plants, division is the easiest way to create an exact duplicate of a parent. I do this in spring or late summer; late summer is best, since flower buds form in early summer. Simply lift and divide the crown, making sure each piece has at least two sets of leaves and both old and new roots. Larger divisions can be put right back into the garden, but smaller pieces should be potted up and watered for about eight weeks, so they can form new roots before they are replanted.

Opposite: *Helleborus torquatus* is a diminutive favorite of many collectors. This particular form comes from northern Italy.

This page: *Helleborus niger*, the Christmas rose, is one of the first hellebores to bloom, but rarely, in this country, at Christmas. Its flowers are as white as a fresh fall of snow.

HELLEBORE CULTURE

When planting hellebores, make sure the crown is just covered by soil. As with peonies, planting too deeply inhibits flower production. Applications of well-rotted manure, leaf compost, and lime encourage strong growth and flowering, but they will forgive you if you forget the applications for a few years.

Flowers of hellebores in the acaulescent group present themselves much more attractively when not surrounded by browning, disfigured foliage from the previous year. The best time to remove the old leaves is in late January or early February, before the flower buds start to push out of the ground. As with epimediums, if the job is neglected until the flower stalks have begun to grow among the old leaves, it actually takes far more care and time. Many a flower has been lopped off by mistake when this pruning is done too late, in haste. In our hillside garden, where hellebores are layered with thousands of snowdrops and early crocuses, we need to get the cleanup done before the bulbs start to emerge from winter dormancy. Since hellebores are a main feature of our early spring garden, their beauty is paramount, and tidying them up becomes a wintertime priority.

In our garden, hellebore leaves do not go in the compost. The leaves take too long to decay—the same waxy coating that helps them hold up through a drought and stay evergreen in the winter also preserves them in the mulch pile. Discarding them also helps us limit the effects of any fungal diseases the old foliage may harbor. Since we try to maintain our garden as mostly organic, rarely using any kind of chemicals, being proactive in disease control is essential.

Opposite: The plants in this group of hybrids called *Helleborus ×nigercors* are crosses between *H. niger* and *H. argutifolius*. The *H. niger* parentage gives the plants better cold hardiness and larger, rounded, outward-facing flowers; *H. argutifolius* brings more flowers per stem and more interesting leaves to the mix.

This page: *Helleborus foetidus* is not particularly long-lived and tends to come up on its own from seed. This plant is one of my favorite hellebore species, even though its common name is a marketing faux pas: Who would want to grow a "stinking hellebore?" (To me, it does not stink; it only has a "catty" scent when the leaves are bruised or cut.)

BREEDING HELLEBORES
THE TRAITS I LOOK FOR

Breeders have their own individual criteria for what constitutes a desirable plant; for me, with hellebores, it is all about the flower form and color. I look first at the flower shape. The sepals or petals should all be uniform, whether rounded or pointed. I tend to like the flowers rounded rather than star-shaped.

I breed away from muddy colors, trying to increase the color clarity and saturation, and also away from green, unless the flower is already green. I like any pattern on the petals, whether edging or striping or spotting, to be consistent and not to look happenstance. I prefer the flowers to be fairly open, because if they are too tightly closed, the markings inside will not be visible.

I breed for a certain coyness, which requires a bit of explanation. I like the pedicel in the back of the flower not to be so short that the flower faces up—such flowers can be ruined if snowed or sleeted on—but not so long and dangly that the flowers hang down like parachutes. I look for ones that are a little more upright, but still hang a bit shyly. Flowers that are completely upright seem unsubtle to me; they do not encourage me to bend down and take another look. The flowers I like best are trying to catch my eye but not staring right at me. With such flowers, I can play magician when I show them off to a visitor—"Now you see it, now you don't!"—as I tilt the flowers up to reveal the beauty they hide inside.

To my eye, hellebores look stalwart and brave when each flower is wearing a pristine white cap of snow.

The following hellebores, which I call 'Brandywine Hybrids', represent a small part of my more than twenty years of collecting and breeding these special plants.

A) It is unusual to find uniform red markings in yellow flowered hellebores, with the same strong red picotee edge.

(B) This particular flower is not white, not pink, but pearlescent and silvery, with a raspberry-colored veining and eye zone.

(C) Silvery gray, almost blue, this plant looks like a misty twilight, and is one step closer to the true blue flower that is the Holy Grail for hellebore breeders.

(D) For me, if the flower is going to be green, it has to be all green. This plant provides a terrific antidote to gray, overcast winter days.

(E) True pink is surprisingly hard to get in hellebores. I strive for an absence of green, whether in light pink or dark pink.

(F) My best black hellebore flower, this little guy looks you right in the eye and says, Hello, spring!

(G) People ask if I like the single or the double hellebores better, and my answer is that you have to have them all.

(H) This double yellow hellebore looks like sunshine, which is often absent at the time of year when it blooms.

(I) When I saw first saw this plant bloom, I thought it was the best thing I had bred up to that time. To me, the flower looks like the frilly, picoteed, hoop petticoat of a nineteenth-century Southern belle.

(J) One of my best yellows, these flowers have a lovely shape, with uniform, rounded sepals.

(K) Darker, more saturated colors, much sought after by both breeders and gardeners, need to be paired with brighter flowers so they show up in the garden.

Witch Hazels

The blooming of the witch hazels (members of the genus *Hamamelis*) is one of the highlights of the winter garden. The plants range in size from large shrubs to small trees, and when February arrives, their branches are clothed with odd, colorful flowers that resemble nothing more than spidery starbursts of shredded colored paper. In another time of year, with more happening in the garden, such subtle blooms might easily be overlooked. But even if one does not see these flowers at first, the spicy fragrance they exude when warmed by even a weak winter sun is unmistakable, and draws one to them as it must surely draw whatever insects serve as pollinators at that frigid time of year.

Three witch hazel species, including *Hamamelis virginiana* and *H. vernalis* which I grow at Brandywine Cottage, are native to the United States; others, including *H. japonica* and *H. mollis*, are Asian species. The various hybrids of the two Asian species, called *H. ×intermedia*, interest me most. Their colors are the most striking, and unlike the fall-blooming *H. virginiana*, they bloom in winter when they can make a significant contribution to the garden.

The flowers of all witch hazels are extremely hardy, holding up to frost, snow, and severe cold. Many also have beautiful fall foliage: rich yellows, oranges, and red can be counted on in many cultivars. For this reason, I try to purchase my witch hazels in the fall when foliage color is at a peak,

Left: *Hamamelis* ×*intermedia* 'Arnold Promise' is a standard-bearer of the genus: the plant is vase-shaped and has vibrant fall foliage.

Right: *Hamamelis* ×*intermedia* 'Harry' was given to me as a memorial plant for my friend Dennis West, whose unusual personality is represented by the distinctively colored flowers.

so I can chose a plant with the brightest leaf color. Since many winter-blooming cultivars are grafted onto the rootstock of the fall-blooming *Hamamelis virginiana*, I also look for plants with no suckers coming from below the graft. With our plants in the garden, we remove any suckers in the fall, when they give themselves away by their out-of-season flowering.

Situating witch hazels is important, both for their vigor and to best appreciate the flowers. They like full sun to part shade: too much shade reduces flowering and results in a leggy plant. Evergreen backgrounds show off the flowers beautifully, and house color can also provide a nice contrast. In our garden, the hillside itself is used as the background. With a good backdrop, the subtle colors can make an effective splash even at a distance, and if you can situate them where you can get a close-up appreciation of the flower and its fragrance, so much the better.

Hellebores and snowdrops make good companion plants for my *Hamamelis ×intermedia* hybrids. For interest later in the season, ornamental grasses that remain upright and attractive in winter can also be used; *Calamagrostis ×acutiflora* 'Karl Foerster' is a favorite of mine. Splashes of yellow also work with darker orange and red witch hazel, either at ground level with *Eranthis hyemalis*, with a yellow-flowered shrub such as *Chimonanthes praecox*, or with the colorful stems of various *Cornus sanguinea* cultivars. *Rubus cockburnianus*, with its stems coated in a brilliant gray-white blooms, also provides a nice contrast to *Hamamelis* selections, but beware of the bramble's ebullient, even invasive nature.

SPRING

When does spring begin? I often ponder: Is it simply a tick of the astronomical clock, when the sun passes a certain point in the sky, or is it more romantic than that? Does it begin when I first smell the earth begin to thaw or see the buds begin to swell? Is it when I first hear the cardinal's mating call, or the honking V-formation of geese as they fly northward? Whenever it begins, it must certainly be before the first daffodil blooms, and well before the dogwoods put on their show. Even though I have seen more than fifty springs in my lifetime, when spring begins it always feels like love at first sight all over again. I feel the sap rising, the excitement of a world shaking off its dormancy and roaring back to life. In spring, a grown man's fancy turns to . . . well, among other things, the garden.

Spring is Mother Nature's way of rewarding us for putting up with the long cold winter, her way of embracing us, taking us back into her warm, loving arms, and each year I submit myself to her willingly and eagerly. At the start of spring, I have no reason not to believe that April showers really will bring May flowers; that the showers and flowers will continue apace through the summer and into the fall; that this gardening season will be the best of my life. The life-sapping heat and drought of summer

Hamamelis ×intermedia 'Pallida' has a paler yellow flower than 'Arnold Promise' and similarly beautiful autumn color. I have several plants on the hillside, which always catch my eye and draw me out into the garden in late winter.

THE ROLE OF SMALL TREES AND SHRUBS IN THE LAYERED GARDEN

When it comes to adding color to a naturalistic landscape, carefully chosen small trees and shrubs can provide a wide range of flowers and foliage in every season of the year. These genera—*Hydrangea, Rhododendron, Amelanchier, Halesia, Magnolia, Hamamelis, Stewartia, Lindera, Cornus, Cercis*—are just the beginning of a long list of such plants that I grow in the garden. As the garden tends to do, it will give us hints about what we should be giving it, and if one plant of a certain genera seems to thrive, I often add more, using different species and cultivars to expand the range of interest and bloom time. These plants often thrive beneath the canopy of deciduous trees or on the woodland's edge, and using them has helped us to recreate the middle layer of woody plants that can be missing from so many gardens, and which we had to remove and replant when we worked on the hillside. In small gardens that may not have enough room for a canopy of trees, these small trees and even larger specimens of some shrubs can become the garden's top layer, with the rest of the plantings scaled down to work with them.

Opposite: (A) The white form of *Cercis chinensis* is a more formal plant than some of the native varieties, but extremely floriferous.

(B) This cultivar of the native redbud, *Cercis canadensis* 'Forest Pansy', has beautiful maroon foliage. The deeper the shade in which it is grown, the more the color of the foliage will fade.

(C) On my dry hillside, where many complex *Rhododendron* hybrids fail, *R.* 'Olga' performs with vigor.

(D) For anyone made weary of the yellow color of common forsythia, *Abeliophyllum distichum* might be just the right plant. Its white flowers are blushed with pink, making it easy to combine with many other plants.

(E) If some evil force made me select just one tree, it might have to be *Stewartia koreana*. The flowers, the multicolored exfoliating bark, the fall foliage, and its graceful branching give it four seasons of interest. When I see it in bloom, I feel like I am in a midsummer night's dream.

This page: The native *Halesia carolina* in the bed named for this moment in April when the tree comes into full flower. Another common name for this plant is the snowdrop tree—no wonder I love its beautiful dangling blossoms.

This page, left: The unfurling fronds of *Matteuccia struthiopteris* combine beautifully with white daffodils.

Right: This colorful yet flowerless composition features the multicolored leaves of an epimedium and the silvery leaves of *Athyrium niponicum* var. *pictum*.

Opposite: Spring invites us to revel in the glories of the season. This bench in the *Halesia* bed is rarely occupied since there is always so much work to do. Sitting in your garden is important, but it is an activity I have yet to master.

are in the future, if they happen at all; my hope is still as fresh as the first leaves on the trees.

I am a creature of the East Coast temperate woodland, and while I might voice the gardener's usual complaints about the weather—too much, too little, too soon, too late—the four seasons are a part of my being, and without them I think I would be very unhappy. My garden is based on these seasonal changes. And probably the changing seasons that I have lived with all my life created my need for change in the garden and in life. Would I appreciate the new life of spring so much if winter, so lifeless by comparison, did not precede it?

While I am a year-round gardener, I must admit that many of my favorite plants bloom in the spring. Hellebores start blooming in winter but finish up in spring. I have loved spring ephemerals like trilliums and hepaticas since I first encountered them as a boy, when tromping through the woods in springtime was one of my greatest joys. Daffodils and tulips bloom in spring, azaleas and dogwoods, magnolias and flowering cherries, and so many more that it is impossible to take them all in, to do anything but lie back and let all the beauty wash over me . . . as if I had any time to lie back in the spring, a season when I get so busy in the garden and with my work that the months can go by in a rush.

In spring I need to force myself to slow down, to appreciate what is there in front of me without thinking of what is to come and what needs to be done. It helps that we have many tours that come through

the garden in spring. While we work like crazy to prepare, I at least get to slow down for the hours of these visits. Opening the garden for tours is one small way of giving back the bounty that has been given to me, and like anything given freely and with an open heart, I often receive much in return. For that brief time, I get to see the garden—really see it, not looking at it critically but instead through a newcomer's excited eyes. Gardens, even though we do them for mostly for ourselves, never look better than when they are shared.

Narcissus

If we consider spring a symphony, then daffodil time is one of the crescendos, with their bright sweeps of flowers stealing the show, trumpeting the definitive arrival of the season. Easy to grow, long-lived, and deer-proof, there are many reasons to love these bulbs of the genus *Narcissus*. As a child I remember picking daffodil bouquets for my mother, and to this day I pick armloads of flowers for inside—which means I always have to buy double quantities for planting, assuring that I will have one bloom for the garden for every one I cut for the house.

Daffodils, which overlap with my later blooming hellebores, were among the first plants I used in the garden for mass planting, and they cheered me on for years while the rest of the garden took shape around them. I planted several hundred each year for the first few years, primarily on the hillside—mostly 'Ice Follies', with a few accents of the large-flowered 'King Alfred' toward the top to draw my eye up the hill. Interspersed among these large drifts, I used smaller numbers of special colors and forms, placed along the pathways to facilitate close-up viewing. Twenty years later, I am still planting daffodils, and if I had to guess how many species and varieties reside in the garden, it would be well over a hundred. While I began with early bloomers, mostly of the cyclamineus group, I am now planting late bloomers to extend the season. I particularly like the antique forms and jonquils, which seem more graceful and more fitting to the age of the house. One favorite is 'W. P. Milner', a nineteenth-century miniature that is smaller than many but, to my eye, far more beautiful than most.

Narcissus are truly easy to grow and about the most reliable plant there is, if certain basic rules are followed. Plant them right side up (large side down), about two times as deep as the height of the bulb, in soil that is not overly moist, in part shade to full sun. The bulbs should feel firm and full; any that are soft and mushy or moldy should be discarded. I remove the spent flowers before they go to seed, a tedious job with my thousands of bulbs but one that provides a variety of rewards. Removing the flowers contributes to strengthening the bulb for the next year rather than letting that energy go to into seed production. It also means that I do not have unsightly sweeps of spent flowers detracting from the later

This bouquet of early miniature narcissus flowers was picked in late March from the garden. For perspective, the vase is barely 6 inches tall.

DYING BULB FOLIAGE

The foliage of bulbs needs to die back naturally to direct the energy of the plant into recharging the bulbs for the following year's bloom. But dealing with this often unsightly mess of brown leaves is a challenge for any gardener. I have found hakone grass and hostas useful for hiding the old foliage of galanthus; hellebore foliage does the same, but this is trickier since both can be in bloom at the same time. When I use bulbs such as tulips in a border, I plant them in the middle or back, so when they finish flowering, their foliage is hidden by the next layer of plants. On the hillside, daffodil foliage is allowed to go down naturally, rather than trimming it off or tying it up in bundles, and since this area is quiet while the foliage fades, I count on any visitor being attracted to the prettier parts of the garden. Daylilies can be used to hide the foliage of daffodils, but the daylily foliage itself has to be hand-groomed as it dies back. In the halesia bed behind the barn, *Matteuccia struthiopteris* effectively hides the daffodil foliage, but care has to be taken to ensure that this vigorous fern does not bury the daffodils alive.

Opposite, clockwise: *Narcissus* 'Double Campernelle' is an old-fashioned plant so radically different from my other daffodils that I had to love it. It was passed along to me by a gardening friend, and therefore doubly treasured. *Narcissus* 'Gipsy Queen' is a miniature with a high cute quotient. The flowers of *Narcissus* 'W. P. Milner' start out with a yellow tint but fade to a papery white. Its detractors say it has too long a neck, but I call that graceful, like a swan. The heirloom *Narcissus* 'Single Campernelle' has a jonquil-like flower, which reminds me of my years in the South, where this form of daffodil is much more commonly grown than it is in the North.

This page, top: *Narcissus* 'Actaea' has captivated gardeners and poets for centuries. I like its simple flowers, and the fact that it blooms in late spring.

Bottom: *Narcissus* 'Mite' is a cyclamineus hybrid, which means it is early flowering. Its long trumpet and swept-back donkeylike ears always make me smile.

spring flowers that are layered among the daffodils and hide the dying daffodil foliage as they grow up.

Daffodils are such a favorite of mine that for a few years I belonged to the Delaware Valley Daffodil Society. I was recruited one time to serve as the scribe for a panel of judges at the society's annual show, and a day spent listening to these experts dissect each entry taught me volumes about what to look for in a flower. Afterward, surveying the entries on my own, I made a long list of bulbs I absolutely had to have. There are thousands of different narcissus in thirteen different divisions. So many daffodils, so little time (and money, and space).

Epimediums

I began planting species and varieties of *Epimedium* because they are among the few perennials that do well in dry shade, which I have more than my share of in the garden. Their tolerance for places where few other plants thrive is made clear in the common name for the genus, barrenwort. As I became more familiar with these little gems, I came to see that hardiness was not all they had to offer. The gentle colors and delicacy of the flowers speak of the freshness of spring like few other plants. In my garden, the epimediums bloom in April and May, after the rush of galanthus and narcissus and coinciding with the bloom of my trilliums, another shade-loving genus with which they often share bed space. The flowers, borne on wiry stems before the leaves fully open, can resemble miniature columbines, or stars, or bishop's hats—the latter another common name.

Epimediums are rhizomatous perennials, more spreading than they are tall, with most growing no more than 12 to 18 inches high. They will thrive in a range of shady conditions, though they do not tolerate poor drainage. Some varieties can form sizable colonies, but the shallow-rooted rhizomes can be kept in bounds and the plants are easily divided and transplanted. The best time to do this work is in autumn or anytime after they flower.

In recent years, I have been captivated by the array of leaf shapes and colors of emerging and mature leaves, which provide as much intrigue as the flowers and over a much longer period, and give me other color and shape notes to play with in my designs. Some species have leaves mottled with red; others have long, pointed leaves, with serrated or spiny edges. Many of the leaves are evergreen or semievergreen, which partly depends on the severity of the winter. I usually cut off the foliage in winter for plants that are not evergreen, and in later winter or early spring for those that are. We do this for the same reason we remove the old foliage of our hellebores, to avoid having the tattered old leaves detract from the beauty of the new foliage and flowers. Tackle this chore before the flowers and leaves begin to emerge, and it can be quickly accomplished with hedge clippers. If you wait a few weeks, it can become a hand-pruning job that is far more tedious and time-consuming.

Epimedium ×warleyense 'Orangekönigin' provides a flower color that is unusual for early spring and is useful in making interesting combinations.

Oppsoite, top left and right *Epimedium* 'Limelight' has a pleasing yellow flower and interesting colorful foliage. When choosing epimediums, I try to get the best of both.

Bottom, left: *Epimedium* 'Enchantress' is one of many plants I have received over the years from Elizabeth Strangman, English plantswoman, who selected and named it.

Bottom, right: *Epimedium fargesii* 'Pink Constellation' has narrow mottled foliage and tiny flowers that look like shooting stars.

This page: *Epimedium grandiflorum* 'Nanum', a diminutive plant with large flowers and striking leaves edged in bronze, won a 1993 Award of Garden Merit from the Royal Horticultural Society in England.

Gardeners who love epimediums owe a great deal of thanks to Darrell Probst of Massachusetts and Robin White of England for their breeding work. Darrell has made numerous collecting trips to China, Japan, and Korea, and both have networked internationally with many other epimedium collectors to amass impressive arrays of species and varieties.

Magnolias

I grew up with magnolias and knew I wanted them in my garden. But what complicates my desire is that I lived both in the north, with a variety of deciduous magnolias, and in the South, with the evergreen *Magnolia grandiflora*. And of course, I had to have both. Fortunately in recent years breeders have created new southern types, like *M. grandiflora* 'Edith Bogue', which are perfectly hardy in my zone 6 garden. I now have about a dozen specimens from both regions, most of them on the hillside, including *Magnolia stellata*, *M. sieboldii*, and *M. virginiana* var. *australis* 'Henry Hicks', which remains evergreen to well below 0°F.

I call magnolias "tree hellebores," in reference to the lovely chalice shape of their flowers that seem to me like oversized hellebore blossoms. The fragrance of some magnolias is wonderful, and the colors on some of the new hybrids are fun to design with. The yellow-flowered *Magnolia* 'Elizabeth' looks striking with the emerging chartreuse foliage of surrounding trees, and I can also use that yellow in combination with ground-level plants, such as black-flowered hellebores or the chartreuse flowers of *Helleborus foetidus*.

Some people avoid magnolias because a late frost can freeze the buds, the result being that instead of a tree laden with glorious bloom, the branches end up burdened with brown. These off-years are infrequent, and the effects of global warming may make them even less frequent. And as with any plant, the on-years make growing magnolias worthwhile. I still remember the spring day when a dark storm sky provided a dramatic backdrop for one of my yellow magnolias in full bloom. If I had gotten a picture it could have been in a calendar or on the cover of this book. As it is, that moment is imprinted in my mind. I would rather have lived with it than lived without it, so I am glad I took the risk and planted this tree; timidity would never have reaped such a reward.

Trilliums

After the late winter rush of snowdrops, hellebores, and daffodils in the garden slows and finally diminishes, I can feel a little let down. Luckily, this time is when many spring ephemerals come into bloom, providing a new flush of beauty in the garden.

Of all the spring ephemeral bloomers, trillium is at the top of my list. I find the effect of these simple three-part flowers to be magical, as they transport me back in time to the mountains of Tennessee, where I first

My obsession with magnolias led me to sacrifice the only sunny part of the hillside, which is now becoming a shade garden because of my collection of these graceful trees. *Magnolia* ×*soulangeana*, with its chalice-shaped pink flowers, looks spectacular underplanted with the green flowers of *Helleborus foetidus*.

Top: The hardy *Magnolia sieboldii*, native to parts of eastern Asia, blooms intermittently through the summer at Brandywine Cottage.

Bottom: *Magnolia* 'Elizabeth' is a notable cultivar with large yellow flowers.

Top: *Trillium erectum* comes with blooms in a variety of colors and variants, from red to white. The white-flowered form is a signature plant in many wildflower gardens.

Bottom: *Trillium pusillum* is called the snow trillium, because it is one of the first to bloom in early spring. The purple foliage fades to green, and the flowers fade to pink.

fell in love with them as a boy. Close to home, a visit to Shenk's Ferry Wildflower Preserve in central Pennsylvania at trillium time, when acres of them are in bloom along with other wildflowers, can be both thrilling and humbling.

In my view, trilliums are the quintessential American wildflower. The eastern United States is home to thirty-five of the forty-eight species, which makes the plant right at home at Brandywine Cottage, and I have planted them all over the garden. Trilliums have a reputation for being hard to grow and their clumps slow to expand. The latter is true, but any difficulty in getting them to thrive is often a matter of planting them in the wrong conditions, or buying plants that might have been wild-collected and not been treated kindly in the process. (Reputable nurseries are always the best source for any plants, especially natives that might be overcollected in the wild. We should make sure that our attempt to bring parts of the native landscape into our gardens is not a case of robbing Peter to pay Paul.)

Trilliums like dappled shade better than deep shade, and they do not like soil that is overly dry or overly wet. Adding organic matter to the soil is helpful, as it mimics their wild habitat with the humus-rich soil of deciduous forests. A plant that is actively growing can be planted anytime, but with dormant plants it is best to wait until fall.

Trilliums are divided into two groups: pedicellate species, which carry their flowers above the leaves and upright, on bent stalks called pedicels; and sessile species, which hold their erect flowers directly on the leaves. For novices to the genus, the white-flowered pedicellate *Trillium grandiflorum* is probably a good one to start with, as it is one of the more vigorous species. Most East Coast species and some of the southern species do especially well in my garden, whereas most of the West Coast species emerge a little too early and can be damaged by late frost.

Good companion plants for trilliums include many other native wildflowers, including the yellow flowers of *Uvularia grandiflora*; the blue, pink, or white flowers of *Phlox stolonifera*; and *Mertensia virginica*, the blue flowers of which would go well with white or pink trilliums. Ferns can add a lacy texture to the bold trillium foliage, and for an exotic combination that is 100-percent native, try growing them with Jack-in-the-pulpit (*Arisaema triphyllum*).

Overaggressive neighbors such as bleeding heart and lily of the valley need to be restrained, because trilliums, like many spring ephemerals, need to have space and light to grow and recharge during their brief time above ground. That time can be even briefer if an early spring heat wave coincides with their bloom. With other plants like my hellebores, which bloom over a long period, I can look at them tomorrow if I get carried away with other chores today, and in fact I can stop and enjoy them any time during the month of March. But trilliums are not called ephemeral for nothing. They need to be appreciated today, because their moment is short, and tomorrow might be too late.

Opposite, clockwise: Trillium chloropetalum 'Volcano', a West Coast species, is one of the few trilliums to be successfully propagated by tissue culture. It has large reddish flowers, and is one of the largest trilliums I grow in my garden. Although the flowers of *Trillium underwoodii* are unusual, the mottled silver and green foliage and the purple stem are also useful in making combinations in the garden. Being taller than some trilliums, it also allows opportunities for underplanting. When I think of wildflowers, I think of *Trillium grandiflorum*. It has a wide distribution in eastern woodlands of the United States, and as we destroy more and more of its native habitat, I think it is a plant that more gardeners should be growing. As the flowers age, they fade to a delicate pink. The silver mottling on *Trillium cuneatum* is variable, so I try to pick out the most strongly variegated plants to add to the garden. The flowers have a fruity fragrance.

NATIVE PLANTS

There are countless beautiful native plants, and I use many in my garden. They link our gardens to the larger "wild garden" by evoking a sense of place. And from an ecological perspective, they can serve as important links in the food chain for local insects, birds, and other wildlife. Native plants—especially those that grow nearby, so-called "local" or "endemic" plants—are also adapted to the location, which helps ensure their success and makes the garden that much more sustainable.

I also enjoy cultivars of native plants— "nativars," if you will—which extend the color range and bloom time of the species and, by being nursery-grown, help relieve the local populations from which native plants are often overcollected.

This page: (left) *Ruellia humilis*, a drought-tolerant perennial that blooms from midsummer to early autumn, makes an effective ground cover for difficult sites.

(right) *Veronicastrum virginicum* takes full sun, blooms in August, and has an upright vertical flower that resembles a thin white bottlebrush. Here it grows with another native, *Phlox paniculata*.

Opposite page: (A) *Erythronium americanum* carpets woodlands with its mottled foliage and bright yellow flowers in spring. Like many members of the Liliaceae, it is a favorite food for browsing deer.

(B) *Pachysandra procumbens* is slower to establish than the Japanese species, *Pachysandra terminalis*, but its large flowers and mottled foliage make it more interesting.

(C) *Wisteria frutescens* is not invasive like the Asian forms of the genus, and in some years it will rebloom.

(D) *Euphorbia corollata* looks like a taller version of common baby's breath (*Gypsophila paniculata*). As with many euphorbias, it has the added advantage of being deer-resistant, and its white flowers combine well with almost anything.

(E) *Dicentra cucullaria*, a spring ephemeral wildflower, naturalizes freely in humus-rich woodland soil.

(F) *Gillenia trifoliata* grows at the woodland's edge, blooms in late spring, and has russet-colored foliage in the fall. The cultivar 'Pink Profusion' is shorter than the species, with pink flowers.

(G) *Veratrum californicum* prefers moist soil. I grow it in dry soil, and so in my garden it is slow to multiply. The flower is striking, but the pleated foliage has a beauty all its own.

USING BULBS IN
THE LAYERED GARDEN

This page: *Crocus sativus* is easily recognized by its bluish-purple flowers and crimson stigmas, which are the source of culinary saffron. It is surprisingly easy to grow.

Opposite: (A) *Camassia leichtlinii* subsp. *suksdorfii* is an underused native plant that contributes 3-foot blue spikes to the garden when it blooms in late April.

(B) I love the elegant, bell-shaped flowers of *Fritillaria persica*, but it can be a challenge to grow. Well-drained soil is a must for its success. To help it get started, I put gravel at the bottom of the planting hole to aid in drainage and I plant the bulbs at a 45-degree angle so they shed water.

(C) *Fritillaria meleagris* will naturalize in damp sites, but it also does well for me in average soil. It has a range of flower colors, mainly reddish purple to black with yellow markings.

(D) *Galtonia candicans*, with spikes of white flowers 3 feet tall in August, is a plant that should be more widely used. It does not need staking, has been hardy for me for several years, and blooms at a down time in my garden.

(E) I use *Corydalis solida* 'George Baker' in both the gravel and ruin gardens as well as in troughs, because it likes good drainage. Even though short in stature, this plant has a saturated color that grabs the eye and carries quite a distance.

(F) *Leucojum aestivum* is a snowdrop relative, with elegant bell-shaped flowers that appear in late spring. It is commonly found in damp areas but is also happy on our dry hillside, where it is beginning to naturalize.

(G) *Tulipa sylvestris* is a sentimental favorite, since it was brought over by Pennsylvania German settlers and can be found naturalized around old homesteads in the state. It grows in part shade, hence the species name, roughly translated "of the woods."

(H) *Cardiocrinum giganteum* is an outsized example of a bulb for shade, blooming from late May into June on flower spikes that have reached up to 5 feet in my garden. Once it blooms, the original bulb dies, but it is easy to keep going from the side bulbs or from seed.

(I) Fall-blooming *Cyclamen hederifolium* is perfectly hardy here in the Delaware Valley. It is a nice counterpoint to the spring-blooming *Cyclamen coum*.

One of the easiest ways to add layers of interest to any garden is with hardy bulbs. They have beautiful (and sometimes unusual) flowers, come in a rainbow of colors, and bloom in all four seasons of the year. They range in size from 6-inch snowdrops to lilies that can tower 6 feet or more. Early blooming bulbs can easily be planted among later blooming herbaceous perennials. Summer bulbs can be an integral part of a July border. And fall bulbs provide welcome color at this challenging time of year.

Many bulbs originated in Asia and the Mediterranean region, making them well suited for my dry garden. Some can even be used in deciduous shade, since they have had their season by the time the tree canopy leafs out. I grow dozens of genera of bulbs, and if I can be allowed a bit of anthropomorphizing, I would say that they are pretty smart critters. They grow, bloom, store up all the energy they need to replenish themselves, and pop out a few progeny—and

(continued)

then, when the weather gets warmer or drier than they like, they go dormant until the following year. If they could only teach other plants to do the same, my garden might not look so forlorn in times of summer drought.

Since I use so many bulbs in my garden and add more all the time, I am lucky that many of them are relatively inexpensive. You can get an especially big bang for your buck with minor bulbs like scilla, and spring-blooming crocus, which if bought in bulk can cost from a nickel to a quarter each, depending on the variety. The cheaper cost allows me to make large gestures with these smaller bulbs, which I then use to justify my purchase of a coveted $50 galanthus. Special galanthus and other rarities get planted along the edge of paths and walls, where they can be more readily seen and appreciated.

I like to plant my bulbs in naturalistic drifts. Some people toss their bulbs and plant them where they land, but I need more control than that. My method is to plant three or five bulbs in a clump, then plant two outside the clump, to make it seem as the bulbs are spreading naturally. I then repeat this arrangement across the area I am trying to fill. With the exception of galanthus, many bulbs do not have to be planted as soon as we get them. Often in the fall, if we are busy trying to beat the frost, cutting plants back and preparing the garden for winter, we will plant bulbs between or after these more pressing chores.

Left: Although examples of the genus *Nerine* are not hardy, we grow them in pots where they create a spectacular fall show, and the containers can be moved wherever we need the color. The pots are allowed to die back and are stored dry in the barn during the winter.

Center: I like members of the genus *Colchicum* because they are both beautiful and deer-proof; I plant more every year. This double-flowered variety is called 'Waterlily'.

Right: In fall bulbs, yellow flowers are uncommon. I count on this hardy bulb, *Sternbergia* species, for that color note in fall. I wonder why people do not plant more of it; perhaps they overdose on yellow daffodils and crocuses in the spring.

LATE SPRING THROUGH SUMMER

As the weather warms up and spring moves into summer, the delicate flowers of the cooler season give way to larger flowers with bolder shapes and colors and, in some cases, delicious fragrances as well. This is the season that comes to mind when people think of the classic perennial border. The garden at this time of year has a fullness and maturity, while retaining the refinement and freshness of plants that have not yet had to struggle against the worst of the summer heat.

To make layers in the garden on the cusp of the summer solstice, the key is to look beyond the stars and create a cast of other characters to work with them. A lead sentence, no matter how beautifully crafted, does not a story make, and neither do I find garden beds full of one type of plant satisfying. Finding the right mix of the right plants in the right place at the right time is always the challenge. This task is always made more difficult because as soon such combinations reach perfection, they start to go over, or get overgrown, or one element dies, and we have to start over again.

I love many garden flowers of this season, in particular, irises, peonies, roses, and lilies. Their timeless beauty remains my horticultural version of comfort food. Some people reject these old-fashioned genera as unsophisticated, but that charge only goes so far. I gravitate toward the

These pictures, taken two weeks apart, show how *Echinops bannaticus* 'Taplow Blue' goes from steel blue in bud to true blue in flower. I appreciate it in both these stages, and later when its seed heads ornament the bed.

old-fashioned and unusual, the single flowered and the subtly colored more than the gaudy, which seem to better fit my personality and the country garden I have created.

Of course, I make exceptions: If a new variety has a color I want, I will often give it a tryout in my garden. I generally have no patience for the disease-prone, often fragrantless hybrid tea roses I knew as a child, but I love the old-fashioned varieties, with their multitude of petals and heady fragrance. The young me marveled at blowsy peony flowers that seemed as big as my head; the plant-obsessed me collects tree peony species and unusual specimens like the yellow-flowered *Paeonia mlokosewitschii*, which would be worth having just for its tongue-twisting name if it were not also one of the most beautiful. My early love of irises landed me years later in a German woodland, in search of *Iris variegata*, about as far from the gardens of my childhood as I ever imagined I would be—but even then I was still in touch with the boy, with his childlike wonder, his innocent reverence for plants and the world in which they live.

This page: As with any large genus, *Lilium* has early, mid, and late-season bloomers. Here *L.* 'Star Gazer', a late bloomer, appears with *Asclepias curassavica*.

Opposite: I love this tall bearded iris 'Rameses'. It was introduced in 1929 but its color is timeless and intriguing.

In this July view of the rose pillar bed, after the roses have finished blooming, *Lilium* 'Citronella' takes center stage along with a supporting cast of thistles and other characters . . . I mean plants.

Irises

According to myth, Iris is the Goddess of the Rainbow, a messenger of the Olympian gods, and wherever she treads on the earth, colorful flowers—members of the Iridaceae—spring up in her footprints. If only planting a garden were as easy as calling on the gods to do all the work. The truth is (and I hope Zeus does not strike me dead for debunking his myth), I have had to plant all my irises myself. I have more than a hundred species and varieties of this plant, which bloom beginning in March with *Iris danfordiae* and continue into July with Louisiana irises. Most irises like full sun; two exceptions in my collection are the shade-tolerant species, *I. cristata* and *I. tectorum*.

If I had to choose a favorite, it might be the antique German bearded irises. I like the form of these heirloom irises more than that of many modern hybrids, which are so stiff and overbred as to appear unreal. And the antique irises seem better suited to my garden. They are more graceful, with papery, parchment-like sheaths around the buds that give them an air of intrigue as they slowly reveal their blooms, like a stripper that slowly drops the seventh veil. On a far more prosaic and practical note, heirloom plants of all types tend to be sturdier than the hybrids (one reason they have survived all these years), which is important since I use almost no pesticides in my garden. Antique irises tend to be more resistant to iris borers (caterpillars that eat their way down through the leaves into the rhizomes, causing them to rot).

Even though they bloom at one of my busiest gardening seasons, I still find time to occasionally hunt for old irises. I visit nurseries that specialize in them, and look for them around abandoned home sites and in old cemeteries. More than once I have knocked on the front door of stranger, to see what the owner might know about an unusual iris that caught my eye. Sometimes I even shamelessly beg a division, and since gardeners are mostly generous, most of the time I get one and make a friend in the process. I enjoy saving these varieties from oblivion, and as they multiply in my garden, I pass them along to others. Sharing favorite plants can be part of a bond of friendship between gardeners, but it is also a form of insurance. If they die out in our own beds, we know where we can get more.

Having said all this in praise of the antiques, one would think I would shun all modern hybrids, but of course I am not that consistent. I buy new irises for my garden every year, and if I see a modern variety with an exceptional color I want to use, I will get it. For a similar reason, I no longer avoid the remontant (repeat-blooming) irises. I used to think they looked out of place in the fall garden, but I have loosened up in recent years and learned to enjoy their encore performances, and to view them as another crayon to use in my late-season combinations.

I began growing *Iris ensata* after a trip to Japan, during which I had a religious experience of the horticultural kind at an ancient Buddhist temple. The monks there had been cultivating iris for more than 500 years,

The native *Iris cristata* was one of the first wildflowers I learned to identify, while on hikes as a child in the Great Smoky Mountains. I now consider it an indispensable player in my part-shade areas.

Opposite, clockwise: Having spent a good part of my growing up in the Volunteer State, I needed to have *Iris* 'Tennessee Gentleman' in my garden. I also appreciate the bronzy-orange color. *Iris bucharica* is an early blooming species that I grow in the sunnier parts of the hillside, in combination with red hellebores. *Iris* 'Wabash' is one of my favorites. Introduced in 1937, it has been a best seller ever since. With *Iris* 'Batik', no two flowers are quite the same. Its unusual color markings raise the eyebrows of purists, but each year I divide it and plant more because its colors work well in the borders around the vegetable garden.

This page, top, left: The color of *Iris* 'Brown Lasso', a recent introduction, proved too irresistible for me to pass up. It looks smashing when underplanted with nepeta.

Top, right: *Iris* 'Indian Chief' has a classic antique form. Its compelling bronzy red falls, with yellow veins and beard, look stunning in combination with yellow flowers and foliage.

Bottom: *Iris ensata* extends iris time into late June. It grows well in both average and moisture-retentive soils.

IRIS CULTURE

I love all irises for the sharply vertical accent of their foliage, although it needs attention to stay looking good. As the summer wears on, I make sure all bloom stalks are cut off, and then remove any shriveled or deformed leaves. Carefully pruning the leaves of surrounding plants is important to give irises the light and air they need. I also try to keep any creeping or self-sowing plants from growing among the rhizomes. This vigilance can be time-consuming if you have even half as many irises as I do, but it will pay off in healthier, stronger, better blooming plants.

Tall bearded irises like full, baking sun: a minimum of seven hours makes them happy. Take extra care to avoid overplanting them. Bearded irises tolerate many soil types, with the exception of wet soils, which they hate and will quickly rot in. If you plant them in average soil and full sun, they will reward you for many years. They are among the easiest perennials to grow.

Blooms in a clump of iris may diminish over time unless the rhizomes or tubers are divided every few years. I do this in early to midsummer, soon after the last blooms fade. I dig out the clump, inspect the plants for borers, and cut away any rotten parts. I divide the plants into smaller pieces, and let the wounds callus over for a day or so. For German irises, I plant the rhizome on top of the ground in a sunny location, burying the attached roots to anchor it. If there is a fan of foliage attached, I cut that back to about 3 inches to keep the rhizome from drying out until it develops its new root system.

and the varieties and colors astounded me. A few years ago I began growing Louisiana irises, which are hybrids of a number of moisture-loving species native to the southern United States, after my neighbors paved their driveway and redirected runoff from their property. This caused problems at first—I had to relocate existing irises and peonies, which would have otherwise quickly rotted—but now I have a dampish spot where the Louisiana irises thrive.

Every time I visit my family near Nashville, I try to take a side trip to Iris City Gardens, about forty miles south in the town of Primm Springs, Tennessee. With seventy-five beds spread out over 10 acres, a visit there always gives me iris overload, especially if I get to visit around Mother's Day, when the flowers are at their peak. I walk through the beds in a daze, making notes about plants that catch my eye, trying not to fall in love with them all. Catalogs and websites are useful tools, but for me nothing is better than seeing plants in person, taking note of their growth habits and making comparisons, smelling them, touching them, and reveling in their beauty. Walking through this nursery and other similar iris gardens is like taking a stroll across a rainbow, and I always have the feeling that the goddess is treading a few steps in front of me, leading her acolyte on.

Peonies

When I was a boy in Reading, Pennsylvania, peonies decorated many a Memorial Day picnic, and their bloom time also marked a good opportunity to visit the gardens of family and friends. And during my childhood years in Tennessee, peonies there were the last hurrah of the spring garden before the hot weather moved in. In both places they were a regular feature in flower arrangements at graduation parties and weddings, because of their sturdiness as a cut flower and because these voluptuous, fragrant blossoms definitely appeal to the heart.

Peonies may be too old-fashioned for some people, but I still love them, not only for the memories they evoke but for the role they play in my present garden. Peonies have sometimes been called roses without thorns, which is about half right, since their flowers are at least twice as large as even the biggest rose. They are versatile, long-lived, and critters like rabbits and deer tend to avoid them. I grow about forty different species and varieties, which decorate the garden in several waves over a six- to eight-week period from April into June.

I grow three different groups of peonies in my garden—the herbaceous types, which include both straight species and cultivars derived from *Paeonia lactiflora*; tree peonies, derived from *P. suffruticosa*, which have a persistent woody framework; and herbaceous types called intersectional peonies, which are crosses between *P. lactiflora* hybrids and tree peonies.

Paeonia obovata is an Asian species that requires shade, unlike most members of the genus. It has two seasons of interest, when in flower (left) and when the ripe seedpods open up (right), and I can never decide which I like best. The blue fruit is fertile: To make more plants, I simply put seeds in the ground around the parent.

Opposite: I love the contrast between the pink petals and the yellow center in the chalice-shaped single flower of *Paeonia lactiflora* 'Nymphe'.

This page, top: With its ice-pink cluster of inner petals contrasting with the darker pink outer petals, *Paeonia lactiflora* 'Pink Cameo' looks stunning in borders.

Bottom: *Paeonia* 'Copper Kettle', an intersectional peony with a color seldom found in the genus, looks especially fine in combination with the similarly colored *Iris* 'Tennessee Gentleman'.

PEONY CULTURE

Herbaceous peonies need to be planted with the crowns just barely beneath the soil. Planting too deeply is a common reason that peonies otherwise properly tended will fail to bloom. Peonies of all types also resent being overshadowed by other plants, which again will reduce their blooming and general vigor. In my rose bed, where peonies are one of several layers, I plant them in the middle of the bed so their foliage is hidden from view, but I need to be vigilant and edit out neighboring perennials to give the plants the light they need to thrive. This chore is one of those that needs to be done in a layered garden where so many plants are grown so closely together, but I would rather spend a little time editing plants than looking at bare soil all summer in my beds.

Peonies are easily grown and their requirements are few, but they respond beautifully to a little attention. They are best planted or moved in the fall. Place them in a sunny, well-drained location. Do not place peonies in the same location where one has been before, unless you remove and replace the soil; this avoids using worn-out soils and reduces the possibility of passing on any peony diseases.

Most peonies like full sun, with the exception of two shade-loving species in my garden, *P. obovata* and *P. japonica*.

Along with other more common perennials, I grow various species peonies in my rose beds, where they provide an early layer of interest before the roses have leafed out and reached their full height. The intersectional peonies bloom a couple of weeks later; among these is *P.* 'Bartzella', the color of which everyone interprets differently—is it apricot, or peach, or peach, or copper?—and which might be more at home on a fashion runway than in a garden. Favorite species in the rose beds include the white-flowered *P. mascula* subsp. *hellenica*, and the beguiling but unpronounceable *P. mlokosewitschii*, with a single yellow flower that looks smashing when underplanted with the burgundy flowers and purple-marked foliage of *Geranium phaeum* var. *phaeum* 'Samobor'. About three weeks after these species have finished blooming, the tree peonies take the stage, with delicate flowers and a stately presence that make them look like a Japanese painting come to life.

The last to bloom are the most common of the genus, the cultivars derived from *Paeonia lactiflora*. These plants were a revered garden flower in China for centuries before they were first introduced in Europe in the late eighteenth century. As with many of the flowers in my garden, I like the single or semi-double forms better than the bodacious double-flowered pom-poms. Besides being more graceful, the flowers with fewer petals also tend to be more upright—one heavy rainstorm and the big pom-poms fill with water and fall over.

Roses

We grow about forty-five varieties of roses in the garden. I long ago decided that these flowers were too beautiful to live without, but as with every genus that has a multitude of forms, I choose them carefully. Regarding the issue of fragrance and roses, people perceive fragrance in different ways, as they do color. I recommend sticking your nose into a rose to see how you personally react to its scent. It is one of life's great pleasures.

I am not a big fan of hybrid tea roses, whose buds and flowers are too stiff and studied for my taste. Many of the older hybrid teas are also prone to a variety of disfiguring diseases that can only be controlled by regular applications of chemical pesticides—off-limits in my mostly organic garden. Breeding for color and form alone—creating large flowers in a variety of odd hues with no fragrance and little disease-resistance— almost destroyed the popularity of these beautiful flowers. I am grateful that a new generation of breeders has pursued disease-resistance as an important trait. Roses like the 'Knock Out', 'Carefree', and 'Hasslefree' series have given the hybrid teas a new lease on life, and brought many more gardeners to roses who had previously avoided them.

While I do grow a few disease-resistant hybrid teas, I far prefer the form of many antique roses, both those with a high petal count and also others with simpler or even single flowers. Some varieties also have interesting thorns and hips, and a few, like the climber 'Iceberg', will flower in light shade. They also tend to bloom before the Japanese beetles emerge, so their flowers avoid being ravaged by these voracious pests. Though many bloom just once a year, to me these heirlooms are more graceful and voluptuous and often more sweetly scented than newer hybrids. The antique varieties also fit better with the old house, and contribute to an aura of romance in the garden. Even the names are romantic: 'Madame Hardy', 'Sombreuil', and the Bourbon rose 'Climbing Souvenir de la Malmaison' evoke the essence of a time long gone, but which we can capture if only for a moment through their flowers.

Among the various types of old roses, I prefer climbers and shrub roses. With shrub roses, I like the plants to be voluminous and ebullient, which means that mine end up taller and wider than most rose growers prefer. To achieve this look, I do not prune them hard at any time of the year. They get lightly trimmed in the fall, when all long canes are removed, and they receive a harder trim in early spring, before the leaves open. To help rejuvenate the plant, I remove any deadwood, any stems that are crossed, and in some years, very old stems. I make my cuts to an outward facing bud, so the rose branches grow outward in a vase shape. This standard pruning approach provides better air circulation, helping to cut down on disease problems.

The arbor at the vegetable garden entrance is festooned with the early June blooms of *Rosa* 'Sarah van Fleet'. A *R. rugosa* hybrid introduced in 1926, it is more vigorous than its look-alike, 'New Dawn'. This view looks back toward the house.

Opposite, clockwise: I love this variety of *Rosa moyesii*, a large shrub rose native to China, for the simplicity of the flower and its large orange hips in the fall. *Rosa* 'Madame Hardy', a fragrant nineteenth-century damask variety from France, is instantly recognizable by its green eye. I only wish it bloomed more, but beauty does have its price. I fell for *Rosa* 'Sombreuil' because of its old-fashioned look and high petal count. Its flowers open a pale yellow and fade to almost white, the color of antique lace. This antique Bourbon rose, 'Climbing Souvenir de la Malmaison', was good enough for Marie Antoinette, so it is certainly good enough for me. It is everything an old rose should be: full-bodied and with a very high petal count.

This page: While I do not grow many hybrid tea roses, I like this one for its soft yellow color that blends well with other roses. It is also disease-resistant, which I require from all my hybrid teas.

Rosa 'Zéphirine Drouhin', a thornless Bourbon variety, has a wonderful saturated color.
I have it espaliered on the fence by the roadside, where it at least serves to slow down traffic,
if not stop it.

Alliums

As an architectural feature, as a vegetable, or as a plant whose ball-shaped flowers make me smile, I find the genus *Allium* (commonly called the onion genus) irresistible. In the vegetable beds we grow leeks, Egyptian onions, chives, garlic, and the white onions so common in supermarket vegetable bins. But we also grow alliums in the ruin and gravel gardens, in containers, and in the borders. I am all for vegetable liberation, letting the edible commingle and cohabit with the ornamental. If chives and leeks (or lettuces or sage or many other edible plants) have ornamental qualities, then I say set them free. Grow them where they look the best— just be sure you have something to fill the hole in the garden if you do end up eating them.

Alliums are easy to grow, tolerant of my heavy clay soil and, being bulbs, tolerant of dryness as well. They are rarely bothered by insects or diseases, and are also among the most resistant of plants to rodents and deer. Maybe these critters, like many humans, do not like having garlic breath.

I grow dozens of different species and forms of *Allium* that bloom from spring into the fall, in colors ranging from white and yellow to blue and purple. I love these plants for the their bold dramatic form, and how they punctuate the garden beds with their ball-shaped umbels of flowers. They combine well with other upright bloomers, such as foxgloves and various salvias, and also look good underplanted with low-growing catmint and forget-me-nots. The larger forms, such as *A. cristophii* or *A.* 'Globemaster', have flowers up to 8 inches across, and are as exciting as the exploding fireworks they uncannily resemble. Using them throughout the garden provides a sense of unity and continuity of form across the various beds.

As with all my favorite plants, I can never settle for just one, or five, or even fifteen: I probably have more than a hundred bulbs of *Allium* 'Purple Sensation', but who is counting? If you are going to use alliums, I say use a lot of them, express yourself fully. Of course, I say this about many plants, but with alliums it is even more important, since just one or a few spotted here and there will end up sticking up out of your beds like a handful of sore thumbs. While they are most often planted in drifts, alliums and other bulbs can also be planted singly, tucked into small holes dug among existing clumps of perennials.

Most alliums are very long lived, and while they can be divided, it is not necessary to do so for them to put on their annual show. Some varieties seed freely, which I deal with by deadheading before the seeds drop. The large flower heads on some varieties dry well and can last about six months. I use them in arrangements on my front porch and other places outdoors, since even when dry, their onion heritage can come on a bit strong inside the house.

Walking through any garden full of large-flowered alliums always makes me feel lighthearted, no matter what heaviness I might have been

Top: *Allium* 'Purple Sensation' is the one I use most commonly in the garden. It is not as expensive as some of the newer hybrids but I find it every bit as effective in the color it provides when planted in mass.

Left: This allium was a pass-along plant from Fred and Mary Ann McGourty, who once ran a Connecticut nursery and wrote extensively about herbaceous perennials.

Right: Common chives (*Allium schoenoprasum*) are not just for the vegetable garden.

This page: I use the large-flowered *Allium* 'Globemaster' sparingly, as an accent. Unlike other alliums, this one has good-looking foliage.

Opposite: *Nectaroscordum siculum* used to be in the genus *Allium*, but whatever the botanists call it, this plant is welcome in my garden for its nodding, graceful, purple-flushed flowers.

Allium 'Mt. Everest' has a standout round shape and white color. I use it as an accent among A. 'Purple Sensation'.

dealing with that day. Seeing all these purple bubbles suspended above the beds makes me think of the old Lawrence Welk Show, on whose set bubbles were often seen floating around—among the dancers on stage, through the closing credits, and around the Hammond organist while she played corny songs like "Bubbles in the Wine."

Lilies

Just thinking about the genus *Lilium* makes me happy. Seeing lilies in flower, and especially inhaling the intoxicating fragrance of some varieties, takes me completely out of my head and transports me to some exotic place—perhaps a tropical island cooled by refreshing breezes of the type we rarely get during southeastern Pennsylvania summers. Such nonvisual sensory experiences—floral fragrance, bird song, and insect buzz, the sweet crunch of a carrot just dug, the crumble of dry soil between your fingers as you pray for rain, the caress of a breeze on your cheek, or the sting of sweat as it drips into your eyes on a hot day when the lilies are in bloom—add layers of depth to our experiences, and bring the garden more fully to life. Unlike roses or jasmine or frankincense, lily flowers contain no essential oils or resins from which perfumers might be able to bottle its magic, making the fragrance all the more elusive and ethereal.

Lilies are the namesake of the Liliaceae, and most gardeners would agree that they are the Queen of Flowering Bulbs, perhaps even the Queen of the Summer Border. They have been grown and adored for thousands of years, appearing in Egyptian hieroglyphics, in several passages of the Bible, and in many Renaissance paintings as a symbol of the purity and chasteness of the Virgin Mary—hence the common name for *Lilium candidum*, the Madonna lily. Roman myth has it that white lilies sprouted wherever drops of the breast milk from Juno, Queen of the Gods, fell to earth while she was suckling the infant Hercules, and the rest of the spilled milk fanned out across the heavens to form the Milky Way.

In my garden, lilies begin to flower after the hydrangeas start to taper off, a lull when I need a star performer, and they fill the role perfectly. With about a hundred species of lilies and countless named varieties in nine horticultural divisions, I have plenty to choose from. I tend to prefer those with a look closer to the species—either long trumpet-shaped flowers with their dramatic, graceful presence, or those grouped under the epithet 'Turk's cap,' because of the more modest (reflected, swept back) look of the martagon's dangling flowers.

The Asiatic hybrids are not my favorite—as with many highly bred flowers, they seem stiff and unnatural to me, with the added demerit that most are unscented. But they are the first to bloom, around the first of June, so I do grow certain colors, including the purple and white 'Netty's Pride', and the unusual butterscotch and raspberry colored 'Kentucky'; these work well in combination with other flowers in the garden's late spring flush. Following are the fragrant, trumpet-flowered *Lilium regale*

Lilium 'Tiger Woods' is striking in its beauty.

and *L. longiflorum* and their varieties. The Oriental hybrids, derived from *L. auratum*, *L. longiforum*, and other species, come next. And the last to bloom are the long, spectacularly fragrant trumpets of *Lilium formosanum*, in early August.

For all their pomp, history, and grandeur, many lilies are surprisingly easy to grow, given a well-drained soil, rich in organic matter, and attuned to their various pH needs. I have found that they like shade at their roots but do not like to be overwhelmed by other plants. Lilies also work well in containers, either as specimens or in combination with other plants. One species, *Lilium formosanum*, is easy to germinate and quick to bloom from seed, sometimes putting out a flower or two in its first season of growth.

Among the Turk's cap lilies I have always admired are hybrids derived from *Lilium martagon*. I tried for years to grow them, with little success, some plants managing to limp along in various places but most just diminishing and eventually disappearing. I had begun to take these failures personally, but finally I learned that these lilies are fussier than some, needing a soil more acidic than my garden can provide. Now, instead of fighting the Battle of the Martagons every year, I grow a host of more congenial Turk's caps that do well for me. I still love these plants (as we often love what we cannot have), but if I want a martagon fix, I visit them in someone else's garden. There I can enjoy them like an uncle enjoys a visit with a favorite niece, content to bask in her presence for an afternoon and then leave the struggle of raising her properly to the parents.

Lilium formosanum is one of the last lilies to bloom, in August. Despite its tall stature and large trumpet flowers, the plants need no staking.

Top, left: When I think of lilies, the form that comes to mind is the trumpet lily, and *Lilium regale* is the queen of the garden when it blooms in mid to late June. It was discovered by plant explorer E. H. Wilson and introduced in 1903. Easy to grow, it is also intensely fragrant.

Top, right: *Lilium* 'Black Beauty' has richly saturated color and gracefully recurved petals. More important, it blooms in midsummer, when early lilies are waning.

Bottom: Many lily fanciers consider *Lilium lancifolium* 'Flore Pleno' an "unlily-like lily" because of its unusual double flowers. I love it because it is unusual, and more coral than other double forms.

KEEPING TRACK OF BULBS

For me, gardening is as much about art as it is about nomenclature or taxonomy, and most of my plants have no labels. This attitude can be tricky when it comes to bulbs, which go dormant and disappear for much of the year. One of the most sickening feelings any gardener can experience is digging a hole for a new plant, only to slice through a clump of forgotten bulbs. For this reason, I do label the snowdrops in my garden, especially the rarer cultivars. With other bulbs (as well as various herbaceous ephemeral plants), a trick I use is to bury several golf tees around the perimeter of the clumps as I plant them. These work like the yellow tape placed on top of buried electric cables or gas lines: when I hit the tees, I know to stop digging. (And, no, I do not play golf, and probably never will, as long as gardening continues to be such an obsession.) Another way I avoid disasters when digging in an area where I think I may have planted bulbs is to use a fork instead of a spade. Then even if I do hit a clump, I am less likely to cut the bulbs in half.

This page: The native *Lilium canadense* has a graceful form. In the wild, it prefers moisture-retentive soils; in my garden it grows well in drier soil, but it does not increase rapidly.

Opposite: I cannot get enough of Turk's cap lilies, and was delighted when I found *Lilium* 'Citronella' so easy to grow.

Hydrangeas

In the garden, the first hydrangeas come into bloom just after the roses fade, in late June, and they continue as a dominant feature in the landscape into August. I have planted dozens in the dappled shade of the hillside, where they anchor a second period of interest in this garden section following the earlier show dominated by the hellebores, snowdrops, and daffodils. Many hydrangeas have colorful fall foliage and flowers that fade and dry beautifully right on the shrub, which extends their season of usefulness well beyond their actual bloom time.

In China and Japan, gardeners have cultivated their native hydrangeas for thousands of years, and I grow a number of these, including *Hydrangea serrata* and a delightful lacecap called 'Tokyo Delight'. Two natives, *H. arborescens* and *H. quercifolia*, are favorites of mine, and I use many plants of the straight species and their cultivars. Especially attractive on the hillside, *H. arborescens* subsp. *radiata* has leaves with gray-haired undersides that can be readily appreciated when viewed from below. I am constantly surprised by how much dryness they can withstand, with the oakleaf hydrangea being especially drought tolerant.

Hydrangeas are divided into two groups by their flower types. Lacecaps have flattened corymbs composed of large, showy sterile flowers radiating around a central cluster of smaller fertile flowers. Mopheads have nearly round heads of large sterile flowers. Both types can appear within the range of cultivars of a single species. For this and other reasons, including the long history of breeding of these plants, the nomenclature of the genus is quite confusing. But I am content, as I am with other genera, to let the botanists figure out what to call the plants I love, and meanwhile, I will continue to use both types of hydrangeas to great effect in my garden.

Just as the nomenclature of the plants is in flux, the flower color of any individual is not even a constant, but instead depends on your soil pH. Some hydrangeas will shift between blue and pink depending on the availability of aluminum in the soil that can be absorbed by the roots. The more acidic the soil, the more aluminum the plant can take up and the more intensely blue the flowers will be. But beware, if you dream of changing your hydrangea flower colors: attempts to radically alter the natural pH of your soil are not usually successful.

I have an affinity for the flowers of lacecap hydrangeas (like those of this large specimen of *Hydrangea macrophylla* 'Blaumeise') because they have a more elegant form than round, ball-shaped mophead hydrangea flowers.

Opposite: *Hydrangea arborescens* 'Annabelle' is a mophead cultivar of our native species, which is naturally a lacecap. Since it blooms on new wood, I cut the stalks of 'Annabelle' to the ground every year. I like the flowers best in their green phase, and use them in combination with orange *Lilium henryi*.

This page, left: *Hydrangea aspera* is a large-growing shrub, with white lacecap flowers and velvety leaves that beg to be touched.

Right: Lacecap varieties can have either single or double flowers, as in the *Hydrangea* specimen plant pictured (which was a gift, unknown name). With a history of cultivation stretching back centuries, hydrangeas have been the subject of much breeding work.

Hydrangea quercifolia 'Snowflake' is a double-flowered form of one of our native hydrangeas.
The maroon autumn foliage of this species is compelling, and the exfoliating bark also provides
winter interest.

AUTUMN

Fall in the temperate climate of our region of Pennsylvania is when the garden comes to the peak of fruition, with the plants voluptuous, blowsy and over the top, sometimes even toppling over. A friend of mine once said that the fall garden has a genteel shabbiness about it, and while the impulse is to get in there with the pruners and neaten it up, there is something to be said for just keeping the paths clear of fallen plants and letting the rest go. Instead of being fearful of this time of decay, it might be best if we simply learned to embrace it as part of the natural rhythm of the life of plants.

If spring has the fizz of a fine champagne, fall is rich and full like a snifter of cognac, a fine way to celebrate the end of summer and the slowing down of the natural world. By fall, the garden is shifting gears, working in a palette of oranges and yellows and russets and reds, the last flashes of light and life for many plants before they lapse into dormancy. I try to echo these hues with my fall plantings, especially in my choice of hardy single-flowered or small-buttoned chrysanthemums, which come in many shades that work well in this season—the soft *Chrysanthemum* 'Sheffield Pink' being one favorite. I also love the unusual flowers of the genus *Tricyrtis* (which has the added plus of growing beneath black walnut), and find that every year I add more fall-blooming crocus and varieties of *Colchicum* to the beds. Asters are another mainstay of the fall borders, along with *Vernonia noveboracensis*, the native ironweed, with its reddish-purple flowers atop stems that can reach up to 6 feet.

As much as possible, we try to embrace the garden as it is passing into dormancy, but find that we can only take so much blowsiness and decay, and end up spending much of our time, before and after the first hard frost, cutting plants down and clearing the slate, especially in the sunny borders around the vegetable garden. While this part of the garden lies quietly until the following spring, our attention moves elsewhere, to the hillside and other areas where the winter plants I love are coming to life.

In this photograph, I not only see the colors of autumn, I can hear the crinkling of fallen leaves as I walk down the path and smell the rich odor of decaying foliage.

Opposite, top: Like many people, I prefer *Amsonia hubrichtii* crowned with its golden fall foliage rather than its spring flowers. Both the *Amsonia* specimen and the blue hardy ageratum (*Conoclinum coelestinum*) are native plants and easy to grow.

Opposite, bottom left: Someone else might view this *Cornus florida* and see a plant at the end of its season, but I see three seasons at once: the fall foliage ready to drop, the bare stems of winter, and the buds that will swell and open into beautiful white flowers in spring.

Opposite, bottom right: *Vernonia lettermannii* 'Iron Butterfly' is an enticing plant for the front of the border, with the same eye-catching flowers as the more common (and much taller) *Vernonia noveboracensis*. Here it grows with *Artemisia* 'Powis Castle'.

This page, top: Containers are changed in the garden to reflect the season. In fall we augment them with gourds and other fruits of the fall harvest, the idea being to create a bountiful horticultural cornucopia. The small green globe in front of the pot is the fruit of a common native tree, *Maclura pomifera*.

Left: In a rare moment, Michael and I are caught standing still in the Brandywine Cottage garden.

Opposite: The delicate pastels of spring give way in fall to the warm vibrant colors of *Sedum* 'Autumn Joy' and several varieties of *Helenium*, in the foreground. The foliage of tropicals provides a bold structure in the looseness of the autumn border.

This page: *Aster novae-angliae* 'Alma Potschke' is an early bloomer in fall. Here it grows alongside *Chasmanthium latifolium*, with a canna leaf as the backdrop.

EVERYTHING IS FAIR GAME

I first saw the Cherry Blossom Festival in Washington, D.C., a few years ago, and it was a spectacular sight. The blooms were barely hanging on, and the slightest breeze or shake of a branch set off a pink snowfall. While the emotional part of me saw the sadness in this moment, the designer in me marveled at the way the petals decorated everything they fell on, lawn and pavement alike. After all, those fallen petals were still flowers, even if they were only hours or days away from being transformed back into the dust of the earth. In my garden, a similar scene occurs ever year when the flowers of the black locust fall on the ruin garden, coating everything in white—a beautiful sight until they brown and dry up and become a distraction that needs to be cleared away.

Just as we celebrate all aspects of a human life, from infancy to the end, why not celebrate all the seasons of growth and life and death in a garden? With certain exceptions that any discerning eye can see (the detraction of dying bulb foliage being one), any moment in a plant's life can have its own particular beauty. As a designer, it is my job to use all those moments, to consider anything that happens in the garden as fair game for my art.

This is especially true in the fall, when so many plants show color and interest in parts other than their flowers. Berries are especially noticeable in fall, such as the white beads decorating the genus *Actaea*, the red of *Ilex verticillata*, or the vibrant purple of *Callicarpa* species. Seedpods, colorful stems, exfoliating bark, drying flowers that refuse to let go, even next year's buds can provide a wide range of opportunities for creative combinations.

People call the dying foliage of trees "fall color" and drive hundreds of miles to see it, but what of the foliage of their shrubs and herbaceous perennials? The bright yellow foliage of some hostas, selections of *Platycodon* and *Polygonatum*, and other plants in fall should be seen as an opportunity to create more interest, rather than just a signal that the end of the gardening season is near. Those yellow leaves would look terrific in combination with blue toad lily, or with blue asters, or the saffron crocus—flowers that, in turn, could also be combined with the reddish-orange tones of the fall foliage of *Hydrangea quercifolia* and *Hamamelis pallida,* or the amber-yellow foliage of *Cornus sanguinea* 'Midwinter Fire'. In making combinations like this, it helps to have an open mind, an ability to think beyond the bloom and relish beauty wherever it is offered.

Top: Just as the fading foliage of fall is fair game for combinations, so is the beautiful new growth of plants in spring, such as the emerging assertive stems of these herbaceous peonies.

Bottom, left: Chrysanthemums are signature autumn plants, but they have more depth when used in combination with other flowers, or in this case, with the bronzy tones of spent lily foliage.

Right: I see these twigs of *Cornus sanguinea* 'Midwinter Fire' through the kitchen window, so even in the dead of winter, I can look out and enjoy their brilliantly colored linear forms.

Asters

Asters are the stars of the fall garden, coming into their own when most everything else is in decline. They are tough, drought tolerant, and combine well with most garden plants, especially with ornamental grasses. With their masses of flowers ranging from whites through blues, purples, reds, and pinks, they work beautifully in contrast to the warmer color tones of autumn. Even though their flowers may be small, their colors are so saturated and jewel-like that they can carry a great distance, appearing especially vibrant in the lower, smoky light of the season. With asters that grow in the woodland, the rock garden, the perennial border, and the meadow, there is hardly a more colorful and versatile plant for this time of year.

Perhaps the most common garden asters are those derived from *Aster novae-angliae*, which is called the New England aster but is actually native to much of the United States. There are many cultivars of this species with beautiful flowers—the salmon-pink 'Alma Potschke' is one of my favorites—but these tall plants, with stems reaching 3 to 4 feet, have a bad reputation because powdery mildew often disfigures their lower leaves. I deal with these asters the same way I deal with my roses: I plant them in the middle or back of the border, where the foliage of other perennials hides their lower foliage. *Aster novae-angliae* 'Purple Dome' is both less susceptible to mildew and half the size of other cultivars, making it a sturdier choice for the front of the border if masses of deep purple flowers are what you want. With many asters, pinching them back around mid-July can make them bushier and less floppy than they might otherwise become.

Lesser known, but to my mind and eye more useful and as beautiful as the New England asters, are species and cultivars of other native asters. One of my favorites is *Aster laevis* 'Blue Bird', with violet-blue flowers from late September into October, on stems that can reach up to 4 feet. 'Blue Bird' is an introduction from the Mt. Cuba Center in Greenville, Delaware, where horticulturists recently concluded an aster trial that highlighted the lesser known types. The results of this study, with their top recommendations, are available on the Internet.

Another favorite is *Aster oblongifolius*, with aromatic foliage that seems more resistant to browsing by rabbits and deer. 'October Skies', with its strong compact mound, and 'Raydon's Favorite', taller and with densely packed blue-purple flowers, are the best cultivars of this species. The native wood aster, *Aster divaricatus*, is a good fall-blooming plant for dry shade. The common form creates a frothy cloud of white bloom, this profusion making up for the tiny size of its individual flowers. Sometimes the color of the flowers can vary, and in a nearby garden I recently saw a blue-flowered form of *A. divaricatus* blooming among a clump of *Polygonatum biflorum*, a native Solomon's seal—a beautiful combination for fall that I

Aster tartaricus 'Jindai', a shorter cultivar of the straight species, is stiffly upright and a vigorous grower.

Opposite, top: Like others of its species, the late-blooming *Aster oblongifolius* 'Raydon's Favorite' is deer-resistant. Its foliage is also more mildew-resistant than other varieties.

Opposite, bottom: *Aster novae-angliae* 'Marina Wolkonsky' grows about 3 feet tall, with mildew-resistant foliage and a striking flower that sings to me from across the garden.

This page, top left: *Aster cordifolius*, the blue wood aster, can grow to 3 feet or more when happy, with each bushy plant covered with hundreds of small flowers.

Top, right: *Aster laevis* is attractive, long-blooming native plant; the selection 'Bluebird' is especially striking. Both the species and cultivar self-sow in my garden, creating a range of handsome progeny.

Bottom: *Aster novae-angliae* 'Purple Dome' is a shorter-growing selection with a stunning, deep purple flower.

hope to duplicate at home. These and other native asters self-sow gently, which suits me fine, since it is one more way I can connect my garden with the greater wild world around me.

Anemones

Anemones are among my favorite plants for the fall border, with rounded blooms that can almost be mistaken for hellebore flowers. In fact these plants are cousins, both belonging to the Ranunculaceae, a family with many members that thrive in my garden. The rounded shape of anemone blossoms is a brisk counterpoint to the general blowsy tendency of many plants in the fall; the fresh blooms help quicken the garden picture even as it is beginning to decline. Fall anemones are taller and have larger flowers than spring-flowering anemones, as if to say, we have the last hurrah!

These herbaceous perennials start blooming in early September and continue through October. In my garden, they prefer part shade, but they can be grown in full sun as long as they get enough water. They are easy to grow "once established"—a phrase that is the key to success with many plants, especially in a temperate climate, where plants that are not "established" (meaning well-rooted) before the winter might have a tough time surviving. The best time to plant anemones is earlier in the season rather than later, but many gardeners, seduced by nursery plants in flower, buy anemones in the fall, when they are putting all their energy into flowers and not into the roots they will soon need to survive their winter dormancy. If you are going to plant your anemones late, make sure to give them extra winter protection—perhaps with a blanket of chopped leaves to protect the crown from heaving out of the ground.

No matter when they are planted, anemones are not the answer for a gardener who needs instant gratification. They will bloom the first year, but they can take a couple of years to "pick up their socks" and make a sizable clump. As with many plants, we can either be patient to achieve the effect we want or buy more plants; in this case I would counsel patience as the preferable (and cheaper) option.

One of the sturdiest anemone varieties is the aptly named *Anemone* ×*hybrida* 'Robustissima', with pale pink flowers on stems that, in ideal conditions, can reach up to 5 feet. Other favorites of mine are 'Honorine Jobert', with single white flowers, and 'September Charm', with deeper pink flowers that can be more than 3 inches across. 'Whirlwind' is a double white, 'Marguerite' is a deep pink semi-double, and 'Lady Gilmour' (also called *A. hupehensis* 'Crispa') has crinkly foliage that gives it textural interest in the months before it blooms.

In the south border, we grow a variety of anemones, combining various shades of pink and plants of various heights so they can play off each other. The darker pinks work best with *Solidago rugosa* 'Fireworks', which explodes into yellow bloom at the same time. But even the lighter pinks can work with 'Fireworks', since all anemones have yellow anthers.

This bouquet of anemones from our garden shows the diversity of flowers, including those of *Anemone hupehensis* var. *japonica* 'Pamina', and three *Anemone* ×*hybrida* varieties, 'Honorine Jobert', 'Montrose', and 'Serenade'. The crinkly foliage at the bottom is from 'Lady Gilmour'.

Unless they are put in too much shade, in which case they may fall over as they lean for the sun, I find that anemones rarely need staking. They wiry stems will lean some even in brighter exposures, but I have learned to call that graceful. In general, I think most plants look better when weaving among their neighbors instead of being hog-tied and corseted into an unnatural upright clump with string and stakes. And in our tightly planted borders, plants like anemones always have someone to lean on.

Opposite: *Anemone ×hybrida* 'Honorine Jobert' grows 3 to 4 feet tall. Its graceful branching stems bear single flowers that are a clean white.

This page, left: The double flowers of *Anemone ×hybrida* 'Montrose' contrast nicely in form to the single-flowered forms that I use more often in the garden.

This page, right: *Anemone tomentosa* 'Berkshire Charm' has a rose-colored, cup-shaped flower and blooms from September into October.

A

B

C

D

OTHER FLOWERS FOR FALL

(A) *Rabdosia longitubus*, a member of the mint family, is an underused plant with electric blue flowers that blooms with the anemones.

(B) As its name suggests, *Helenium* 'Sahin's Early Flowerer' blooms before most others in this genus, from late summer into early fall. It can be forced to flower later by pinching it back in early June.

(C) *Helenium* 'Double Trouble' is an unusual double-flowered variety. Unlike other heleniums, this one holds its foliage; others tend to lose their lower leaves and get "bare knees," which is why it is best to plant them mid-border.

(D) I like Korean chrysanthemums because they bloom late and will even take some early frost. Taller and looser then overbred supermarket mums, I prize and collect many different color variants, which augment my palette of fall combinations.

(E) *Leonotis leonurus*, a tender perennial in zone 6, has an orange flower that works well in autumn combinations. Its unusual flower shape also adds interest.

(F) There is a wide range of species and cultivars of the genus *Tricyrtis*, but so far I have resisted the temptation to start a collection. I do grow a few, including *T.* 'Sinonome', which I appreciate for its unusual flowers and the fact that it will live beneath my black walnut trees.

E

F

FALL GALLERY TWO
SEED PODS AND BERRIES

(A) *Asclepias tuberosa*, a host plant for monarch butterflies, reveals its seeds in October, just before they take flight from the pod.

(B) Native Americans ground the seeds of *Chasmanthium latifolium* to make an edible mush. Perhaps that would be one way to control this plant's aggressive nature.

(C) Flowers of the genus *Smilacina*, which are white with a hint of green, are beautiful and especially fresh looking in spring. And the plant's richly colored berries extend the plant's interest into late summer and early autumn.

(D) The bright berries of *Callicarpa dichotoma* are in sharp contrast to the yellow *Helianthus salicifolius* flowers behind them.

(E) The seed heads of *Angelica gigas* are slow to shatter, and the stems of this summer bloomer stay upright well into autumn.

(F) Variegated pokeweed (*Phytolacca americana* 'Silberstein') is not for the faint of heart, but I always say that if you are going to have weeds, you may as well have pretty ones, and this one is native besides. I try to remember to cut off and discard the berries before they drop and reseed.

E

F

When I began this garden twenty years ago, I wanted it to incorporate all the elements: earth, water, wind, and fire. And thus, the fire pit, toward the northeast corner of the property.

WHAT IS BEAUTY?

WHEREVER I GO, MY EYES ARE WORKING OVERTIME, and always in the back of my mind is the question, "What is beautiful?" Many gardeners have a stilted definition of beauty, having been lectured at too often about what we are *supposed* to find beautiful. But I am an equal-opportunity seeker of the sublime, grateful to appreciate it wherever I find it.

In my work, I do a lot of traveling, sometimes abroad but much of it on the roads between Maryland and Connecticut, my sales territory for Sunny Border Nurseries. Over the years, I have seen some grand gardens, both in this country and others—the gardens of royalty, castles, and country houses. I am certainly glad to have had these experiences. They have given me more inspiration than I could ever put into my garden, even if I lived nine lives. But I can just as easily be inspired by simpler scenes closer to home.

In nearby Lancaster County, I see Amish vegetable gardens, so simple yet so elegant and beautiful that I cannot help but pull over to get a closer look. Once while sitting in my car in front of such a garden, I had a roadside epiphany of sorts. I had always thought that beauty in a garden was all about plants and how we used them, and that certainly is a big part of it for me. But it is also about the love a gardener expresses in tending a space—love for the plants, love for the family that will be eating the plants, love of beauty for its own sake—love that radiates out into the world and draws empathic folk right off the road, to sit at the wheel and soak it in.

On one particularly memorable day, I was driving a back road on my way to a nursery and saw a front-yard combination that stopped me dead. On both sides of a sidewalk leading up to the front door, the gardener had underplanted orange daylilies and purple liatris with yellow coreopsis, using yuccas in full bloom as eye-catching sentinels at either end. This combination could have been at the White House; it could have been a double border leading to the front door of a castle. I have to thank that anonymous gardener, because the moment she or he created will feed me for a lifetime.

Though I saw nothing in this front yard garden that was poised to take the stage after this combination had faded, in that moment it was perfect—and when you get down to it, these take-your-breath-away moments are what gardening is all about, what we are all trying to create. Maybe not just one moment—the more time and thought we put into it, the more layers and nuance we pack into our gardens, the more of these moments we can string together. But life, after all, is lived only one moment at a time. The rest is history, or in the unknowable future. Perhaps because I have been near death twice, or maybe just because I am a perennial optimist, I have learned to pause and appreciate each moment as it comes, for what it is.

This beautiful moment in the garden relies entirely on the color, shapes, and textures of foliage.

SOME OF MY FAVORITE GARDEN BOOKS

Armitage, Alan. *Herbaceous Perennial Plants*. Champaign, Illinois: Stipes, 2008.

Beales, Peter. *Classic Roses*. New York: Henry Holt, 2002.

Bishop, Matt, Aaron Davis, and John Grimshaw. *Snowdrops*. Maidenhead, U.K.: Griffin Press, 2006.

Case, Frederick W., and Robert B. Case. *Trilliums*. Portland, Oregon: Timber Press, 2009.

Cubey, Janet. *RHS Plant Finder 2011–2012*. London: Royal Horticultural Society, 2011.

Dirr, Michael A. *Dirr's Hardy Trees and Shrubs*. Portland, Oregon: Timber Press, 1997.

Dirr, Michael A. *Hydrangeas for American Gardens*. Portland, Oregon: Timber Press, 2004.

Druse, Ken. *The Natural Shade Garden*. New York: Clarkson Potter, 1992.

Fish, Margery. *Cottage Garden Flowers*. London: B. T. Batsford, 2001.

Hansen, Richard, and Friedrich Stahl. *Perennials and their Garden Habitats*. New York: Cambridge University Press, 1995.

Hinkley, Daniel J. *The Explorer's Garden*. Portland, Oregon: Timber Press, 2009.

Hobhouse, Penelope. *The Country Gardener*. London: Frances Lincoln, 2000.

Jekyll, Gertrude. *Wall, Water and Woodland Gardens* New York: Macmillan, 1982.

The white form of *Cercis chinensis*.

Jekyll, Gertrude, and Lawrence Weaver. *Gardens for Small Country Houses*. Charleston, South Carolina: Nabu Press, 2010.

Lane, Chris. *Witch Hazels*. Portland, Oregon: Timber Press, 2005.

Lawrence, Elizabeth. *A Southern Garden*. Chapel Hill: University of North Carolina Press, 2001.

Lloyd, Christopher. *The Well-Tempered Garden*. Weidenfeld & Nicolson, 2003.

Ogden, Scott, and Lauren Springer Ogden. *Plant-Driven Design*. Portland, Oregon: Timber Press, 2008.

Oudolf, Piet. *Designing with Plants*. Portland, Oregon: Timber Press, 2008.

Page, Russell. *The Education of a Gardner*. New York: Random House, 2007.

Rice, Graham, and Strangman, Elizabeth. *The Gardener's Guide to Growing Hellebores*. Portland, Oregon: Timber Press, 1993.

Robinson, William, and Rick Darke. *The Wild Garden*. Portland, Oregon: Timber Press, 2009.

Thomas, Graham Stuart. *Perennial Garden Plants*. London: Dent in association with Royal Horticultural Society, 1982.

Thomas, Graham Stuart. *Three Gardens of Pleasant Flowers*. Deer Park, Wisconsin: Capability's Books, 1983.

Verey, Rosemary. *The Flower Arranger's Garden*. New York: Sterling Publishing

ACKNOWLEDGMENTS

Gardening has been the best common denominator in my life; as I always say, it's not just the plants but the people you meet. Over several decades in the horticultural world, I have been influenced by far too many people to list them all here, or even remember them all. I am most grateful for the support of my family—to my parents, David G. and Bobbie Jean Culp; and their parents, the Rev. L. T. and Katherine Culp and John and Irene Thorpe, who invited me into their gardens at a very young age; to my sisters, Linda Lee Oliver and Sherri Lee Culp, for their love and support through the years and during this project; and to Michael Alderfer, without whom the garden at Brandywine Cottage would be a very different, and much lonelier, place.

When I decided to pursue horticulture as a career and return to school, I met three very important people in my plant life: Stephanie Cohen, my herbaceous plants instructor; Gail Neiman, co-worker at Waterloo Gardens; and Joanne Walkovic, co-founder of the Hardy Plant Society/Mid-Atlantic Group, the organization that gave me a home in horticulture and whose members continue to provide me encouragement and knowledge. Joanna Reed both taught me a way to garden and introduced me to some of the dearest people in my life. Elsie DuPont has shared her enthusiasm and love of plants and garden design, and has been a wonderful companion on many plant collecting trips. Alastair Gunn has both shared my passions and encouraged me to take up new ones. Bill Thomas has been a great friend and supporter over many years; both the gardens and the gardeners at his current venue, Chanticleer, continue to inspire me. The gardens of the late Christopher Lloyd at Great Dixter, now evolving so beautifully under the care of Fergus Garrett and his staff, are another source of inspiration.

Thanks to Jane Pepper, Chela Kleiber, Marilyn Romanesco and the staff of the Pennsylvania Horticultural Society, who have done so much good for the green world for so many years. Claire Sawyers and the staff of the Scott Arboretum at Swarthmore College are an example of what higher education truly should be. Elizabeth Strangman, Gisela Schmiemann, Günter Jürgl, John Massey and Kevin Belcher of Ashwood Nurseries, Will McLewin of Phedar Nursery, Robin and Sue White of Blackthorn Nursery, and Thierry Delabroye educated me in the ways and wiles of the world of hellebores. John Grimshaw, Alan Street, Hitch Lyman, Louise Peters, and many others, helped turn me into a full-blown galanthophile.

Tom Fischer of Timber Press encouraged me to write this book, and made it possible for me to work with what I call my "dream team"— co-author Adam Levine and photographer Rob Cardillo, whose crafts-manship I admire and whose friendship I cherish. These two became as dedicated to the book as I was, and for that I will be eternally grateful. I would also like to thank Ellen Wheat, Eve Goodman, and Mike Dempsey for their thoughtful editorial contributions to the book.

Linda Oliver, Tom Borkowski, Queenie Northrup, and Carol McCo-nomy read and commented on early drafts of the text, and Gail Furman typed my notes for this book. Thanks to Sue Leary, The Chanticleer Foundation, and the Blue Café in Downingtown, for providing us work space during the course of the book's creation.

Thanks also to Pierre Bennerup, Marc Laviana, and Kathy Bonomi, of Sunny Border Nurseries; Tony Avent; Michael Bowell; John Bryer; Alma Nelson Cassel; Steve Castorani and North Creek Nurseries; Charles Cresson; Marie Ducharme; Nancy and Bill Frederick; Heidi and Rich Hesselein; Dan Hinkley; Nancy and Bob Holman; Sally and Dick Lighty; John Londsdale; Marian and Jeremy Martin; Leah, Adrian, and Sebastian Martinez; David Mattern; Diane Mattis; John McIntyre; Deborah Miles; Dixie Northrop; Lauren Springer Ogden; Robin Parer; Graham Rice; the Russell family of Russell Gardens; Betty Sparks; Martha Stewart; Marco Polo Stufano and the staff of Wave Hill; Mary Ann Thomas; Dave Thompson and the Continuing Education staff at Longwood Gardens; and members of the Winterthur Garden and Landscape Society.

Finally, my thanks to gardeners everywhere: you make our world a kinder, gentler place.

INDEX

A

Abeliophyllum distichum, 212, 213
Acanthus, 44
Acanthus spinosus, 49
Acer griseum, 183
Achillea, 43
  'Coronation Gold' and 'Moonshine', 43
Acorus gramineus, 104, 105
Actaea, 281
  'Brunette', 58
Actaea pachypoda, 62
Adonis, 180, 199
Adonis amurensis, 186, 187
  'Flore Pleno', 179
Agastache, 44, 100
  'Blue Fortune', 62
Agave, 50, 62, 100, 101, 109, 144, 145
ageratum, 277
Alchemilla mollis, 138
Allium, 50, 91, 95, 110, 112–115, 128, 129
  'Globemaster', 256, 258
  'Mt. Everest', 260–261
  plant portrait, 256–262
  'Purple Sensation', 256, 257, 260–261
Allium cristophii, 256
Allium karataviense, 95, 108
Allium schoenoprasum, 256, 257
alpine plants, 111
alyssum, sweet, 127, 128, 129, 138
Amaryllidaceae, 66

Amelanchier, 212
Amsonia hubrichtii, 32, 149, 276, 277
Anemone
  'Honorine Jobert', 286, 287
  'Lady Gilmour'/*hupehensis* 'Crispa', 286, 287
  'Marguerite', 'September Charm', 'Whirlwind', 286
  plant portrait, 286–289
Anemone hupehensis var. *japonica* 'Pamina', 286, 287
Anemone ×*hybrida*
  'Honorine Jobert', 286–289
  'Montrose', 286, 287, 289
  'Robustissima', 149, 286
  'Serenade', 286, 287
Anemonella, 176
Anemonella thalictroides f. *rosea* 'Oscar Schoaf', 178, 179
Anemonella thalictroides 'Green Hurricane', 176
Anemone robustissima, 150, 151
Anemone tomentosa 'Berkshire Charm', 289
Angelica gigas, 293
angel's trumpet, 118
animals, 155–157
annuals, 32, 127
Aquilegia, 199
arborvitae, 70
Arisaema triphyllum, 229
Artemisia 'Powis Castle', 276, 277
Arum italicum, 60
Aruncus, 86

305

Cordyline, 81

Coreopsis, 298

Coreopsis tripteris, 62

Cornus, 38, 39, 77, 82, 155, 168, 185, 212, 214

Cornus florida, 168, 276, 277

Cornus mas, 64

Cornus sanguinea, 211
  'Midwinter Fire', 80, 81, 180, 181, 280, 281

Cornus sericea, 100
  'Flaviramea', 192

Corydalis, 51

Corydalis cheilanthifolia, 51, 100

Corydalis lutea, 91, 108

Corydalis solida, 105
  'George Baker', 51, 234, 235

Corylopsis, 96

Cotinus, 149

Crocus, 51, 180, 204, 234, 274

Crocus pulchellus, 27

Crocus sativus, 234, 281

Crocus tommasinianus, 27, 51, 192

Cupressocyparis leylandii, 70

Cyclamen, 82

Cyclamen coum, 190, 191, 192, 234, 235

Cyclamen hederifolium, 234, 235

Cypripedium, 82

Cypripedium parviflorum, 64, 176, 177

D

daffodils. *See Narcissus*

deer/deer-resistant plants, 66, 70, 216, 245, 282, 285

Dicentra, 51

Dicentra cucullaria, 230, 231

Dicentra formosa, 86

Dicentra spectabilis 'Gold Heart', 16, 18, 82

Digitalis, 44, 110–113, 118, 122–123, 127, 130, 176, 256

Digitalis purpurea, 130

disease-resistant varieties, 67

Disporum, 60, 132, 168, 170
  'Dancing Geisha', 82, 169

dogtooth violets, 81

dogwood. *See Cornus*

drifts, 234

driveways, gravel, 91–95

drought tolerant plants, 62, 82, 83, 86, 91–93, 220

Dryopteris, 86

Dryopteris ×australis, 62

E

Echeveria, 100, 101, 108, 109

Echinacea, 62

Echinops bannaticus 'Taplow Blue', 235

edelweiss, 105

Edgeworthia chrysantha, 185, 186, 187

elephant ears, 118, 150, 151

endemic plants, 230–231

entertainment spaces, 88–89

entry gardens, 82–91

Ephedra, 62

ephemerals, 149, 166, 214, 229, 266

Epimedium, 62, 64, 86, 149, 198, 204, 214
  'Enchantress' and 'Limelight', 222, 223
  plant portrait, 220–224

Epimedium fargesii 'Pink Constellation', 222, 223

Epimedium grandiflorum 'Nanum', 223

Epimedium ×warleyense 'Orangekönigin', 220, 221

Eranthis, 180

Eranthis hyemalis, 29, 211

Ericaceae, 60

Erythronium, 81, 166

Erythronium americanum, 230, 231

Eucomis, 105, 109

Eucomis comosa 'Sparkling Burgundy', 14, 15

Euphorbia corollata, 138, 230, 231

Euphorbia cyparissias, 96, 104, 105

Euphorbia 'Diamond Frost', 62

Euphorbia dulcis 'Chameleon', 62

Euphorbia griffithii 'Dixter', 62

Euphorbia hypericifolia 'Inneuphe' ('Diamond Frost'), 108

Euphorbia ×martinii, 18, 104, 105
  'Ascot Rainbow', 14, 15

Euphorbia milii, 108

Euphorbia palustris, 62, 138

evergreen screen, 70, 72–73

F

fawn lilies, 166

fences, 70, 71

fennel, bronze, 125

ferns, 49, 81, 86, 109, 132, 219, 229

fertilizer, 61

forest grass, Japanese. *See Hakonechloa macra*

forget-me-nots, 52–53, 112–113, 118, 127, 256

forsythia, 212, 213

foxglove, 44, 110–113, 118, 122–123, 127, 130, 176, 256

'Potter's Wheel', 199, 203
Helleborus ×*nigercors*, 203, 205
'Pink Frost', 18, 108
Helleborus orientalis, 192
Helleborus torquatus, 199, 202, 203
Helleborus vesicarius, 199
Hepatica, 86, 166, 199, 214
Hepatica japonica, 166
Hepatica transsilvanica, 166
Hermodactylus tuberosus, 176, 177
holly, 127, 192
honeysuckle, 42, 146–147
Hosta
 companion plants, 60, 198, 219
 in containers, 111
 in layered garden design, 49, 51, 149, 168, 170
 maintaining foliage, 127, 281
Hosta cultivars
 'Blue Cadet', 86
 'Mouse Ears', 'Sum and Substance', 'Zounds', 51
Hosta sieboldiana, 51, 158, 159
Humulus lupulus 'Aureus', 104, 105
hyacinth, summer, 62
Hydrangea, 185, 212, 268–273
 'Tokyo Delight', 268
Hydrangea anomala subsp. *petiolaris*, 62
Hydrangea arborescens, 268
 'Annabelle', 270, 271
Hydrangea arborescens subsp. *radiata*, 268
Hydrangea aspera, 271
Hydrangea macrophylla 'Blaumeise', 268, 269
Hydrangea petiolaris, 80, 81, 182, 183
Hydrangea quercifolia, 171, 268, 281
 'Snowflake', 272–273
Hydrangea serrata, 268
hypertufa troughs, 106, 107

I

Ilex 'Blue Princess', 127
Ilex verticillata, 100, 281
insects, 64, 65, 67
Iris, 44, 62, 64, 105, 111, 118, 122–123, 149, 235–236
 'Batik' and 'Wabash', 242, 243
 'Brown Lasso' and 'Indian Chief', 243
 Louisiana, 149, 244
 plant portrait, 240–244
 'Quaker Lady', 236
 sibirica (Siberian), 127
 'Tennessee Gentleman', 242, 243, 247
Iris bucharica, 242, 243

Iris cristata, 111, 240
Iris danfordiae, 240
Iris ensata (Japanese), 149, 240, 243, 244
Iris tectorum (Japanese roof), 86, 240
Iris variegata, 236
ironweed, 274

J

Jack-in-the-pulpit, 229
Jasminum nudiflorum (winter), 180, 185
jewel box, 77–82
Joe-Pye weed, 118
Juglans nigra, 57, 59–60, 132, 274, 291
Juniperus virginiana, 76

K

Kniphofia, 44, 64, 138
 'Ice Queen', 138
kohlrabi, 118, 119

L

ladybugs, 64, 65
lady's slipper orchids, 64, 176, 177
Lavandula (lavender), 138
Lavandula stoechas, 100
lawns, 60–61
leeks, 256
Leonotis, 44
Leonotis leonurus, 291
Leontopodium alpinum, 105
Leucojum, 149
Leucojum aestivum, 234, 235
lewisia, 105
Leyland cypress, 70
liatris, 298
Ligularia dentata 'Desdemona', 149
Liliaceae, 66, 230
Lilium (lily), 62, 66, 110, 111, 122–123, 219, 235–236, 298
 'Black Beauty', 265
 'Casa Blanca', 122–123
 'Citronella', 238–239, 266, 267
 'Kentucky' and 'Netty's Pride', 262
 plant portrait, 262–267
 'Star Gazer', 236
 'Tiger Woods', 262, 263
 'Turk's cap', 262, 264, 266, 267
Lilium auratum, 264
Lilium canadense, 266
Lilium candidum (Madonna lily), 262

soil amendments, 61, 77, 166
Solanum quitoense, 129, 130, 147
Solidago, 62
Solidago rugosa 'Fireworks', 149, 150, 151, 286
Solomon's seal, 27, 29, 168, 169, 281, 282
spiders, 65
spruce trees, 82–83, 86
spurge, 62, 96, 104, 105
squill, Siberian, 81
Stachys macrantha 'Superba', 44
Stachys officinalis, 65
Sternbergia, 234
Stewartia, 212
Stewartia koreana, 212, 213
Stylophorum, 51
Styrax japonica, 158, 159
succulents, 62, 100
sun-loving plants, 62
sweet alyssum, 127, 128, 129, 138
Symphyotrichum, 62
Symphytum azureum, 2–3, 4, 63, 171, 172, 174

T

Tanacetum niveum, 100
texture, 44–50, 54, 55, 125
Thalictrum, 51, 199
Thalictrum rochebrunianum 'Lavender Mist', 125
Thermopsis, 44
Thermopsis caroliniana, 129
thistles, 111
Thuja 'Green Giant', 70
toad lily, blue, 281
Trachelospermum jasminoides, 62
Trachystemon orientalis, 176, 177
Tradescantia 'Sweet Kate', 96
trees, 56–60, 212–213
Tricyrtis, 60, 274, 291
  'Sinonome', 291
Trillium, 64, 81, 86, 149, 166, 214, 220, 224,
  227–229
Trillium chloropetalum 'Volcano', 228, 229
Trillium cuneatum, 228, 229
Trillium erectum, 227
Trillium grandiflorum, 228, 229
Trillium luteum, 38, 82
Trillium pusillum (snow trillium), 227

Trillium underwoodii, 228, 229
troughs, 106–107, 110–111
Tulipa (tulip)
  deer eating, 66
  in gravel, 91, 94, 95
  in layered garden design, 82, 111, 127–130, 132,
    155, 214
  maintenance, 219
  planting, 37–39, 42
Tulipa cultivars
  'Little Princess', 95
  'White Triumphator', 82, 129, 130, 149
Tulipa linifolia 'Bright Gem', 96
Tulipa sylvestris, 234, 235

U

unity, 19, 37, 50–53, 92–93
Uvularia grandiflora, 229

V

vegetable garden, 111–124
Veratrum californicum, 230, 231
Verbesina, 62
Vernonia, 111, 149
Vernonia lettermannii 'Iron Butterfly', 276, 277
Vernonia noveboracensis, 274, 277
Veronicastrum virginicum, 230
vertical gardening, 44–49, 50, 146–147
Viburnum rhytidophyllum, 63–64

W

wall utilization, 54, 55, 77
walnut, black, 57, 59–60, 132, 274, 291
water features, 134–135
water use, 60–61, 62
weeding, 64
well house, 84–85, 86
willow trees, 56–57
winter aconite, 29, 211
wintersweet, 180
Wisteria frutescens, 4, 6–7, 230, 231
witch hazel. *See Hamamelis*

Y

yarrow, 43
yucca, 298

·BRANDYWINE·CO

driveway
gravel
garden

halesia bed

jewel box

ruin
garden

BARN

formal
hellebor
garden

entry
garden

COTTAGE
circa 1790

roadside bed